VINDICATING TRUMP

DINESH D'SOUZA

Since 1947
REGNERY
An Imprint of Skyhorse Publishing, Inc.

Regnery books may be purchased in bulk at special discounts for sales promotion, corporate gifts, fund-raising, or educational purposes. Special editions can also be created to specifications. For details, contact the Special Sales Department, Regnery, 307 West 36th Street, 11th Floor, New York, NY 10018 or info@skyhorsepublishing.com.

Regnery® is an imprint of Skyhorse Publishing, Inc.®, a Delaware corporation. Visit our website at www.regnery.com.
Please follow our publisher Tony Lyons on Instagram @tonylyonsisuncertain.

10 9 8 7 6 5 4 3 2 1

Library of Congress Cataloging-in-Publication Data is available on file.

Jacket design by SP & JB and David Ter-Avanesyan
Back jacket photograph courtesy of the author

Print ISBN: 978-1-5107-8324-9
eBook ISBN: 978-1-5107-8325-6

Printed in the United States of America

For Marigold Gill
We fight, so that our America, can be your America too.

CONTENTS

INTRODUCTION:
A MOST UNUSUAL MAN

———————

Destiny is not a matter of chance; it is a matter of choice; it is not a thing to be waited for, it is a thing to be achieved.[1]

—William Jennings Bryan

I have met four presidents, and closely studied another three, and Donald Trump is the most interesting and unusual of the group of them. There are different ways to take this—his critics would say Trump is unusual in his dictatorial proclivities, or in the volume of crimes he has committed—but I mean it in the most straightforward way. Trump is the most unique and intriguing figure in our time, perhaps in the whole landscape of US presidential history.

For all their differences, the others all fit a pattern, and Trump doesn't. He breaks the pattern. To use a term Trump never would, he's sui generis. There's no one like Trump, there never has been, and I venture to say there never will be again. When God made Donald Trump, he threw away the mold.

Let's look at three examples of Trump's uniqueness. When Trump's former attorney general Bill Barr, who had been castigating Trump since the two men fell out over the issue of fraud in the 2020 election, unexpectedly announced he would vote for Trump in 2024, Trump skipped entirely over Barr's rationale—"I think the real threat to democracy is the progressive movement and the Biden administration"—and responded this way:

> Wow! Former A.G. Bill Bar, who let a lot of great people down by not investigating Voter Fraud in our Country, has just Endorsed me for President despite the fact that I called him "Weak, Slow Moving, Lethargic, Gutless and Lazy" (*New York Post*!)....Based on the fact that I greatly appreciate his wholehearted Endorsement, I am removing the word 'Lethargic' from my statement. Thank you Bill. MAGA 2024![2]

In January 2018, Trump posted on social media: "North Korean Leader Kim Jong Un just stated that the 'Nuclear Button is on his desk at all times.' Will someone from his depleted and food starved regime please inform him that I too have a Nuclear Button, but it is much bigger & more powerful one than his, and my Button works!"[3]

Can you imagine any other US President saying this? Can you imagine anyone else calling the North Korean dictator "Rocketman"? And yet Trump met that year with Kim Jong Un at the Singapore Summit—the first of three meetings—and the two men got along; the North Korean leader was quite evidently charmed and impressed by Trump.

Just recently, Trump said at a Michigan rally, "All Kim Jong Un wants to do is buy nuclear weapons and make 'em....I said just relax—Chill! You've got enough. Let's go to a baseball game—we'll go watch the Yankees."[4] What a way to communicate with one of the world's most notorious despots! Any other political leader would have talked about nuclear deterrence and "making significant progress" in this, or "expressing our concerns" about that, and blah, blah, blah. Not Trump! Here we get a window into his personal style of diplomacy. He seems to think the hair-trigger North Korean nuclear threat might be mitigated, if only a bit, by putting Kim Jong Un in a baseball cap.

Finally, consider Trump's reaction to the attempted assassination in July 2024. A bullet grazes him on the ear, splattering blood on his face. There are multiple sounds, which means multiple rounds have been fired. There could, as far as anyone knows, be multiple shooters. Trump ducks down, and is engulfed with Secret Service agents, but then immediately he says "Wait!" and pops back up. His face is defiant in a manner reminiscent of his mugshot. He raises his fist in the air. He says, "Fight! Fight! Fight!" The stunned audience responds with bellowing chants of "USA! USA! USA!"

Now what normal person, in such a perilous situation, instinctively responds that way? Trump's photo, which will likely go down in history as one of the most iconic photos since Iwo Jima, owes its resonance to the wondrous and astounding inner strength of the man. Lots of people think of themselves as brave, resilient, tough as nails. But we can never know—and they themselves can never know—to what extent this is true until they are subjected to an actual test. Trump demonstrated his bravery in a manner that could not possibly be anticipated or rehearsed. Dana White, founder and CEO of the mixed martial arts UFC, has said on more than one occasion that Trump is the "greatest badass" he has ever seen and also "the greatest fighter of all time."[5]

It's not easy to assess this exceptional man. Is he such an unconventional leader that conventional standards cannot be used to measure him? Or is he a conventional leader in an unconventional time, when the old standards no longer apply? One thing should be clear: I'm evaluating Trump in terms of his suitability for becoming, once again, President of the United States. His temperament, his personality, his judgment, his character all matter insofar as they cast light on his fitness to assume, for the second time, the helm of the country and the leadership of the Western world.

This is the question now before the American people, while the world watches with apprehension. There is a huge debate around Trump, or more accurately, this is a man who provokes extreme reactions. I confess to being a partisan here, a Trump enthusiast, a champion of the MAGA movement to "make America great again."

But I wasn't always this way. My background is that of a Reaganite, who worked in my twenties in the Reagan White House. For most of my career I've been at think tanks like the American Enterprise Institute and the Hoover Institution at Stanford University. Most of my colleagues there became Never Trumpers—strenuous advocates of "anyone except Trump." I myself was not an early passenger on the Trump train, and I defected to his side in 2016 only when he became the official Republican nominee.

So my current enthusiasm about Trump is not the product of early infatuation, but of considered judgment. It is the result not of prejudice, but of experience. At the outset, therefore, I thought it helpful to spell out my dealings with Trump, to help the reader understand where I'm coming from, and also to see Trump up close, in order to compare the public and the private man.

I first met Trump in early November 2019, when he invited my family to the White House. This, by itself, might seem surprising. A year and a half earlier, on May 30, 2018, I received a presidential pardon from Donald Trump. I had been convicted of a campaign finance violation, donating $20,000 of my own money to a college friend who was running for the US Senate in New York. That alone is a fascinating story—one that I have told elsewhere. Check out my book *Stealing America* for the juicy details![6]

But the point is that I had done my sentence—eight months overnight in a confinement center, paid a hefty fine, even did mandatory psychiatric counseling, supposedly to enlighten me to the admirable qualities of the system that went after me. Still, the felony label hung around my neck, and the Left routinely and delightedly tormented me with it in the media and on social media. Trump's pardon erased all that, fully restoring my rights and placing me into the strange category of being an "ex-felon." I was a felon, in other words, before felony became cool.

How, one might ask, does one go about getting a presidential pardon? Many people assume that I previously knew Trump, that he somehow owed me, and that he was repaying me for doing him a big favor or for supporting him in his presidential campaign. None of this was true. I didn't know Trump, I hadn't done him any favors, and I was not an early supporter of his campaign.

I had spoken to Trump once previously on the phone. That was two years earlier, in the 2016 campaign, right before one of his debates with Hillary Clinton. I was at Liberty University to deliver a convocation address, and the president of the school, Jerry Falwell, who was close to Trump, asked me what Trump should ask Hillary in the debate. I said I had two questions that Trump should unload on her.

Before I could tell him what they were, Falwell was on his cellphone, calling Trump. "I'm here with Dinesh D'Souza," he said, "and he has two questions he wants you to use to skewer Hillary." I told Trump what they were. First, I asked him to challenge Hillary to explain how the Clintons went from being broke to being worth hundreds of millions of dollars. "How do you become a multimillionaire on a government salary?" My second question was, "Hillary, will you admit that the Democratic Party was the party of slavery, of segregation, of Jim Crow, of the Ku Klux Klan, of lynchings and racial terrorism, and the party that opposed the Civil Rights Amendments that permanently ended slavery, extended equal rights under the law to all citizens, and gave Blacks the right to vote?"

Trump loved it. "That's great," he said. "My people are terrible. Write up those points, will you, and send them to Steve Bannon." I said I would do it, and I did. But then Trump never used what I sent. He raised the first issue in his characteristic roundabout way and he didn't bring up the second one at all. Trump! I shrugged and pretty soon forgot about the whole thing. That was the full extent of my interaction with Trump, prior to the pardon which came two full years later.

Senator Ted Cruz, as it turns out, is a big part of this story. My wife, Debbie, who headed a large Republican women's club in the Houston area, was good friends with Cruz. Ted and his wife, Heidi, invited us to dinner at their home in Houston. This was in April 2018. On our way there Debbie and I discussed the bad blood between Trump and Cruz, which arose out their rivalry in 2016, when Cruz was the second highest vote getter in the GOP primary. Trump had called Cruz "lyin' Ted" and, even more memorably, suggested that Ted's father Rafael Cruz, the pastor who married Debbie and me, might have been involved in the assassination of JFK. Yes, there had been a rumor to this effect, but it was preposterous!

"Don't bring up the question of a pardon," I warned Debbie. But a couple of hours later, after dinner, as I chatted with Ted's young daughters, I noticed that Ted and Debbie were animatedly talking, and I overheard Ted say, "What can I do for you guys?" To which Debbie replied, "You have to ask Trump to pardon Dinesh." Before I could intervene, Ted replied, "I'm seeing him next week at the NRA convention in Dallas. I'll ask him." Whoa! You can imagine Debbie's and my conversation on the way home. But Debbie insisted, "Ted wouldn't do it if he didn't think Trump would listen."

A few days later, my phone rang. It was Ted. He said he was in the limousine with Trump and his chief of staff, John Kelly, in the back. Ted leaned over and said, "Mr. President, you pardoned

Scooter Libby and that was a good thing. Now you should pardon Dinesh D'Souza." And Ted reported that Trump scratched his chin and replied with a single word, "Done." Then he turned to John Kelly and said, "Make it happen."

I found this astounding on two counts. Not only had Trump established a cordial working relationship with a former foe—letting bygones be bygones—but in addition I could not think of any president who would come to a decision on such a big matter so quickly, even impulsively. Having worked in the Reagan White House, I had some idea of how these things worked. Presidents typically take up pardon proposals with an advisory team. They hash out the pros and cons. If necessary, they summon a "focus group" in order to anticipate the public reaction. But in this case, Trump, who didn't know me and owed me nothing, made his decision on the spot.

"Don't get too excited," Cruz cautioned me. "There has to be a legal review. It takes a few weeks. Things can get held up. But don't worry, my office will stay on it. In the meantime, say nothing to anyone. Let the process play out." Debbie and I kept our silence, and exactly 30 days later, Cruz called again. I could hear the excitement in his voice. "The White House just called me," he said. "They asked for your phone number. This is very good news. It means the President is going to call you. But keep your cell phone on. You must be ready to take the call. You don't want to be trying to call them back."

Two hours later, I heard the White House operator, "Mr. D'Souza? Hold for the President of the United States." It was Trump, and what followed was a very Trumpian conversation indeed. "Hey Dinesh," Trump said, "I'm here with John Kelly. You know John Kelly, don't you?" I said, "No, I know he's the chief of staff, but I don't know him." How would I be expected to know John Kelly?

Trump continued, ignoring my response, "Now about your

case—I knew from the beginning it was total bullshit." I resisted the temptation to laugh. "Bullshit," I knew, is one of Trump's favorite words. He routinely calls out bullshit in his rallies. He sees bullshit everywhere in politics, and not entirely as a spectator; he's a bit of a bullshitter himself. Trump, one might say, is a connoisseur of bull-shit. And by bullshit here he meant that while I had indeed exceeded the campaign finance limit in 2012, he knew it was a technical vio-lation that normally brings a warning and maybe a few weeks of community service—but in my case, the Obama justice department went after me because I had just made a highly successful film *2016: Obama's America* exposing the vindictive narcissist in the White House. The idea that I was being fairly and proportionately pun-ished for what I did was bullshit.

Trump and I talked about some other things, and he praised my work and influence on behalf of freedom. But I suddenly realized I wasn't listening to him. How bizarre! I'm having a one-on-one con-versation with the President of the United States, for the first time in my life, and I'm not paying attention. The reason, of course, is that I was highly attuned to the subtext. I was paying attention to what Trump was not saying.

With Trump, conversations sometimes have a subtext. You have to notice the dog that didn't bark. And here the subtext was the underlying rationale for the pardon, which Trump knew and I knew, even though it never came up in our conversation. And seeing this was, for me, the most exhilarating part of that brief exchange. In pardoning me, Trump was delivering a giant Up Yours to the Obama administration!

Almost as an afterthought, Trump said, "I'm going to give you a pardon tomorrow morning." He added, "Don't say anything about it publicly. Get ready, because the press will be all over it. But don't say anything until I tweet about it." I chuckled and agreed. I loved the idea of my pardon being announced, not by official White House press release, but by a presidential tweet by a man who had already established himself as a true artist of the medium.

The next morning, my pardon was headline news. I remember going on Anderson Cooper's CNN show where he tried to embarrass me by suggesting that only on account of knowing some very powerful people—Ted Cruz, Donald Trump—was I now off the hook. I reminded him that only on account of pissing off some equally powerful people—Barack Obama, his "wing man" Eric Holder—was I on the hook in the first place.

All of this was in my mind when I stood with my family in the Oval Office, awaiting our meeting with President Trump. We were taking in the ambience when the door burst open and Trump entered, beaming. He immediately recognized my daughter, Danielle. "Hey," he told her, "I just retweeted you." She replied, a thrill in her voice, "I know." He laughed. "I saw your beautiful face," he said, "and you have such a great way of expressing yourself."

We sat down on the two sofas across from Trump's desk. Trump sat in his chair and beckoned me to an unoccupied one. "You move over here, Dinesh. Come sit next to me. We're going to have you sit in the dictator's chair. I call it the dictator's chair." Right away we launched into the topic of contemporary politics. "It's crazy out there," Trump said. "The other side is relentless. Crazy. Totally dishonest."

My wife Debbie talked about Venezuela, where she was born. She showed Trump before-and-after photographs of her aunt who lived there. (She has since passed away.) In the "before" picture Judi Cestero looks portly, well-fed, happy. In the "after" picture—after socialism, that is—she looks gaunt, emaciated, her face worn from strain. Trump studied the two photos and blurted out, "What a way to lose weight!"

That's Trump in his witty, unpredictable mode. Debbie wasn't sure whether to laugh. She had been trying to make a serious point. But I assured her that Trump had gotten the point, yet he couldn't resist responding with a one-liner. Trump's one-liners are so memorable that we talk about this one, even years later, and his diehard fans are a virtual encyclopedia of them. You can be sure his foes— the targets of the one-liners—have also never forgotten them.

Debbie thanked Trump for the pardon. "It was the right thing to do," Trump said. "You didn't even ask for it, but I did it. And look! Now they are trying to do the same thing to me that they did to you." Trump paused. "But I fight back. I have the means to fight back. Like you fought back. We have to. These people are disgusting. They never stop." This was in November 2019, a month prior to Trump's first impeachment. But it was a long way from his criminal indictments. It's haunting to see how Trump, even then, foresaw the lengths to which the Democrats would go to take him down.

I said we were no longer in the Reagan years, and the relative civility and decency of those years was now a thing of the past. Debbie said, "Mr. President, I see you how are attacked all over the place, nonstop, without any kind of restraint or respect for the office. Frankly, I don't know how you do it." At this point, the two of us expected Trump to say, "Ha, ha, ha. Whoop-de-doo. It's fun for me because I couldn't care less what they say."

But Trump didn't say that. "Well," he said, leaning forward, "to tell you the truth, it gets to me after a while. I'm out there trying to get the job done, and no matter what I do, these people are after me." Trump had just directed one of the most successful antiterrorist operations, resulting in the death of the world's number one terrorist, Abu Bakr al-Baghdadi, as well as his second in command. In scale, it resembled the Bin Laden operation carried out under Obama.

Yet while Obama's action was greeted with hosannas and cheers—the media went into full genuflection mode—Trump's action received an entirely different response. "They act like it was nothing. It was a one-day story. And even then," Trump said, with a tone of disbelief, "all they wanted to talk about was the dog. For them, it was all about a meme."

Our talk turned to impeachment. "It's such a sick joke," Trump said. "There was nothing wrong with that call," referring to his call with Zelenskyy about potential Biden corruption in Ukraine. Of course Trump has subsequently been more than vindicated, since we now know the Biden family cashed in to the tune of millions of dollars at the time when Joe Biden was vice president and Obama's point man for Ukraine.

"I'm really lucky to have the transcript," Trump said. "If I didn't have the transcript, all these people, these Never Trumpers and all these dishonest people, they would come forward and make up all this stuff, and say I said things I never said, and there would be no way for me to prove what I actually said." Trump had no way at the time of knowing the Democratic House would indeed impeach him, although the impeachment vote failed in the Senate.

I looked over at my wife Debbie, and I noticed she was close to tears. We thought Trump didn't care one whit about what people said about him. But now we saw a side of him that was hurt, uncomprehending, vulnerable. Without quite intending it, Trump had showed us his human face. If only, Debbie said later, the American people could see that side of him. I said he probably didn't want them to see it.

We talked about many other things—forty-five minutes of just him and us in the Oval Office—from India to Venezuela. He gave us his personal insights into Putin, Xi, Modi. What struck all of us about the meeting was how congenial he was, and how candid. He wasn't arrogant. He wasn't self-absorbed, as he is typically portrayed in the press. He looked us in the eye. Later, my daughter would say he was so "real," which I took to mean authentically American, authentically himself. "People tell me they love his politics but not his personality," she said. "But I love his personality. It inspires me to stand strong in my beliefs, even when I am treated badly because of them."

I told Trump I had just one piece of advice to give him, and it concerned what he should do after the presidency. "You should start a news network. Not another Fox News Channel. Another CBS or NBC. A network that reaches 50 million, not 5 million people." He looked at me, contemplating, I suppose, what his life would be if he got out of the real estate business and went into the news business. "You are one of the few people," I told him, "who could pull this off."

Then the White House photographer took photographs. Before it was over, the president invited us to the White House lawn to watch him take off in his helicopter to a rally in Kentucky. There we stood, with the wind beating against us, watching this intrepid fighter for the restoration of his country's greatness, with a task ahead of him greater than that which faced Reagan, lift off into the air and disappear gradually into the clouds.

Three years later, in 2022, the mood of the country was entirely different. Covid struck in early 2020, wrecking the Trump economy, and making it much more difficult for him to coast to re-election. The 2020 election, which we were assured was "the most secure election in US history," was in fact one of the least secure, with a plethora of rule-changes, improper interventions such as Mark Zuckerberg dumping half a billion dollars to infiltrate election offices and bankroll mail-in dropboxes, anomalies upon anomalies, improbabilities upon improbabilities. Biden won, but millions of people, Trump included, were convinced the election was rigged and stolen.

In 2022, with the help of the election integrity group True the Vote, I made the film *2000 Mules*, which for the first time documented the fraud. We used two foolproof methods to demonstrate how the Democrats rigged and stole the election: cell phone geo-tracking, and the official surveillance video of the mail-in dropboxes taken by the states themselves. Since we intended to rent Mar-a-Lago for our movie premiere, we decided to show the film to Trump in advance.

My immediate family was there, and also a couple of members of my film team. Catherine Engelbrecht and Gregg Phillips from True the Vote were also present. We watched the film with Trump in the screening room, and he sat almost motionless, which is out of character for him. "It's a brilliant work," he said to me afterward. "It's going to be your biggest success ever."

That's Trump—he thinks in terms of ratings and success. He reminds me of Achilles in Homer's *Iliad*. Achilles wanted Briseis as his concubine because she was his prize—she represented the public acknowledgement that he was indeed the greatest warrior among the Greeks. Achilles was incapable of saying to Agamemnon, "You keep Briseis. I know that I'm the greatest warrior among the Greeks." Trump, like Achilles, seeks external validation for his projects. In this respect, his values are those of the ancients, not those of the moderns.

After the screening Trump said, "It's a great film, but it's a bit too long. You should shorten the last part." I said the last part was necessary because we had to cover what could be done to prevent the fraud. "Oh, you don't need to cover that," Trump said. "Just show the fraud. Let other people figure out what to do about it."

I reflected on this for a moment, and instantly I knew that Trump was right.

Very rarely does anyone give me a movie suggestion that I actually take. The reason is that I have a top-flight film team, and we are good at what we do, and outside suggestions are often quite outlandish, or at the very least options we have already considered and rejected. But here Trump was saying, in effect, "We've just watched *The Shawshank Redemption*. Do we really want to have a panel discussion at the end on how to correct the abuses at Shawshank? No. That's anticlimactic. Also, it's not the job of a movie. Let the movie do its work, and let the people who fix prisons do what is necessary to correct the abuses exposed in the movie."

So I made a mental note to cut a big chunk of the last part of the film. This would make it cleaner, tighter, with a more powerful climax. Trump also said, "Nowhere in the film do you say the election was rigged and stolen." I said, "I know, but I imply it was." He said, "It's always good to say it." I said I would think about it. Trump shook hands and said, "All of you should stay for lunch." And while we were eating lunch, I felt a slight tap on my shoulder. Someone pressed a little Post-it into my hand. I turned around, expecting some old Mar-a-Lago golfer, but it was Trump. The Post-it said, "The election was rigged and stolen." I shook my head and laughed. I agreed to say as much in the movie and added a line to that effect.

Trump also attended our movie premiere in the great Mar-a-Lago ballroom, with eight hundred guests in attendance. Most of them were conservative media and social media influencers. Trump wanted Mar-a-Lago members to come, so we had a couple hundred of them as well. We count on the media and social media invitees to watch the movie, go nuts over it, and convey that enthusiasm to their audiences. Trump had agreed to say a few words, and he spoke in his characteristic whimsical manner, and the crowd loved it!

But then, unexpectedly, he came and sat down next to me to watch the movie. I say "unexpectedly" because we knew, and the audience knew, he had already seen it. Still, I think he wanted to show his support, and he also wanted to see it again. This time, however, he gave a running commentary while the movie was playing, and it had several hilarious tidbits, so I feel obliged to share a couple.

Being familiar at this point with the content, Trump focused his attention on the technicalities. "The music," he said, at one point. "How did you get the music? Did you buy it? Did you have someone compose it?" I told him we had a movie composer, Bryan Miller, who has done our music for several films. I reminded myself at this point that Trump has been, for most of his life, a major cultural figure. He starred on *The Apprentice*. He's been in movies. He pays attention to how these things come about.

Then in the same vein, Trump said, "Your voice! Dinesh, you have a very good movie voice."

I said, "Thank you."

Trump rubbed his chin. "It's a good thing you have a voice," he said, "because if you didn't, you'd have to hire someone else to do the narration."

I chuckled and admitted this was true.

Since *2000 Mules*, I've been in closer touch with Trump, meeting with him at the Trump golf facility in Bedminster, New Jersey, texting him from time to time. Every time I see him, he recalls my pardon and he usually tells me the same story. "You know, I pardoned Scooter Libby, and I pardoned you, but that Scooter Libby is not a good guy. Can you believe that, soon after I pardoned him, he went to a fundraiser for Liz Cheney? Liz Cheney! My people asked him about it, and he pretended to be shocked. What's the big deal, he said. He doesn't think it's a big deal. So I'm reconsidering the wisdom of pardoning that guy. He's a rat. But I'll always be glad I pardoned you."

Earlier this year I called him to ask a favor. But I got his answering machine, so he called back at one a.m., when I was fast asleep. "This is your favorite President," he said. "Call anytime."

My purpose in calling was to ask him to endorse my son-in-law Brandon Gill, who is running for Congress in Texas congressional district 26, in the northern suburbs of Dallas. The longtime congressman, Michael Burgess, decided not to run, so my son-in-law decided to enter the race. The district is a red, pro-Trump district where a victory in the primary pretty much guarantees election to Congress.

That's why the Trump endorsement was critical, and naturally every candidate was angling to get it. Trump had met Brandon a couple of times, and he knew that Danielle, my daughter, was the youngest board member of Women for Trump in 2020. Trump asked about the other candidates, and I briefed him. He agreed to endorse Brandon. "I'm doing this for you, Dinesh," he said. "Don't forget me."

Here I admit I thought of the opening scene of *The Godfather*. I felt, momentarily, like the undertaker who had come to ask a favor, and was being granted it, on the condition that someday he might be called upon do a little service in return. Trump is transactional in that way, and he's also a guy who values loyalty. He gives it, and he expects it.

From time to time during the primary campaign, Trump called me to ask, "Is our man going to win?" I said, "Absolutely." Trump knew, of course, that Brandon is only thirty. He was in an eleven-person primary with a mayor, a senior congressional aide, the son of a longtime former congressman from that district, Dick Armey, and several others. In Texas, you have to get over 50 percent to avoid a runoff. "It might be a runoff," Trump warned me. "In that case, I'll help to get him over the finish line."

"We're trying to avoid a runoff," I told Trump. But my confidence was shaken when a Never Trump PAC dumped over $2 million in ads against Brandon at the last minute. The ads were ridiculous and over-the-top. They depicted Brandon as a New York tycoon, since he worked for a few years on Wall Street; as a Chinese spy, since one of the banks he worked for was Nomura, which does transactions worldwide; as an advocate of Defund the Police, since Brandon was an executive producer on my film *Police State*, which exposes the abuses of the FBI and other intelligence agencies.

Even so, these ads ran every single day, many times a day, on both radio and TV stations throughout the greater Dallas area. Fortunately, Brandon and his team were able to counter with ads of their own, stressing Brandon's Trump endorsement. Brandon was also endorsed by Senator Ted Cruz and a range of Texas congressmen. Still, how do you get over 50 percent in an all-man race with a $2 million ad spend against you?

Brandon showed he could do it. When the results came in, he got 58 percent. The next highest vote-getter got around 14 percent. So Brandon got 58, and the other ten candidates put together only managed 42. Trump was elated. He called Brandon to congratulate him. He chatted with Danielle. Then, when he heard I was visiting, he said, "Give me the Master."

Brandon and Danielle howled in amusement. "He calls you the Master," they said, handing me the phone. Trump said he knew we could pull off the win, and he said that it contributed to his amazing record of endorsement wins. He gave me the tally, an impressive number, which I forget. A couple weeks later, he called again to convey his high hopes for Brandon in Congress, and to give me his revised endorsement tally, another unbelievably high number, which I also forget. Trump only acknowledged a single loss, in Texas, where the house speaker, Dade Phelan, narrowly fended off a challenge to retain his seat.

Most recently, I texted Trump about my *Vindicating Trump* movie project, and said it would not be the same without his participation. I wanted to interview him one-on-one, and ask him questions different from the ones he usually gets. Trump texted me back, "WOULD BE MY GREAT HONOR." All caps! But given Trump's legal woes and insane campaign schedule, it was difficult to get the interview on the calendar. As May went by and June came along, I was getting frustrated. But then it happened at Mar-a-Lago in the third week of July, just a few days after the attempted assassination attempt and immediately following the Republican Convention. And in a way that proved fortuitous. Had I interviewed him earlier, the interview would have seemed somewhat incomplete or at least dated. Now I feel like I just did it the day before yesterday! (You can watch the interview in the movie, of course, or read the transcript for yourselves in the Afterword.)

I had forty-five minutes for the interview. We went forty-five minutes straight, and then Trump aide Margo Martin started waving her hands wildly. "Time's up." And so we stopped. We had covered what I intended to cover. Trump evidently was expected to rush to another meeting. But Trump, being Trump, said, "Let's take some photographs." We did, and then Trump launched into a fascinating monologue about some of his GOP rivals—Ron DeSantis and Nikki Haley—who eventually came over to his side. Then we got into a discussion about the mental incapacity of both Joe Biden and Kamala Harris—Trump doesn't think Kamala's intellect is any more impressive than Biden's. To my amazement, this conversation lasted another forty-five minutes, and then Trump sauntered off to his next appointment.

I convey these episodes in order to be fully transparent about my relationship with Trump, and also to convey aspects and dimensions of the man that I don't think come through in his media coverage— no surprise—or in his public persona. With Reagan, the private and public persona were the same. With Trump, this is not the case. Moreover, while Reagan was a "peacetime general," and in my view the greatest president of the twentieth century, Trump is a "wartime general," seeking to lead a nation that is in the middle of a cold civil war.

Context matters, and the relevant context is that this most unusual man, Trump, is now running once again for the presidency at perhaps the most unusual period of American history, when the country is in a mess and also divided perhaps more than it was in Lincoln's time. Trump's seemingly impossible task is to get us out of the mess and put the country back together again. He must, if he can, restore a greatness that now seems lost and almost irretrievable.

CHAPTER 1

THE ENIGMA OF TRUMP

A riddle, wrapped in a mystery, inside an enigma.[7]
—Winston Churchill

The purpose of this book is to resolve the mystery of Donald Trump, but before I can do that, I have to persuade you that there is something mysterious about Trump that needs to be resolved, so that we as Americans can determine his eligibility to be the forty-seventh president of the United States. Trump, who has been a major figure on the American scene for decades, seems such a familiar figure that most people think they've figured him out.

But sometimes our leaders are right there before us, yet there is something about them that eludes us. In an earlier book I considered the puzzle of Reagan: "How an ordinary man became an extraordinary leader."[8] Many people said what made Reagan so successful was that he was such an ordinary fellow, yet ordinary fellows don't restore the economy of a nation, revive its patriotic spirits, and also, along the way, win the Cold War "without firing a shot," in Margaret Thatcher's memorable words.

Years later, I sought to resolve the enigma of Barack Obama. Obama, unlike Reagan, emerged out of nowhere. Even so, by 2012

1

he had been president for four years. Still, the media portrayed him as a civil rights icon, a fulfillment, if you will, of Martin Luther King's dream. It was difficult to understand America's first Black president in any other terms.

Yet, as I showed in two books and my first documentary film *2016: Obama's America*, Obama's real story had nothing to do with Selma or Montgomery. His dream came not from Martin Luther King but from his father, a Luo tribesman who became a passionate anti-colonialist, suffused with hatred for America and the West. Read my books on Obama, and watch the film, and my conclusions will now seem commonplace. At the time, they provoked fierce resistance not only from the Left but also some quarters on the Right.

With Trump, we have not just a single enigma but rather two of them. To borrow Churchill's phrase, uttered in 1939 to describe the Soviet Union, Trump is a "riddle wrapped in a mystery inside an enigma." First, how can the same man inspire such intense and radically opposed reactions? Imagine that you and I are sitting in a café and we see an accident on the street. We would be expected to differ somewhat in our accounts of it, but at the same time, our accounts could not be radically incompatible, because after all we have both witnessed the same accident. Yet with Trump, his fans and his haters seem to inhabit alternative universes, at least with regard to their apprehension of the man.

We saw this chasm emerge with the reaction to the assassination attempt on Trump. His supporters were mortified. His critics were not. Some of them were openly jubilant on social media. Even some Democratic political candidates could not conceal their wish that the assassin's bullets found their intended mark. Of course the media, which is by and large in the hater column, moved quickly to solemn calls for all sides to "dial it back." Yet this was quite obviously a fake evenhandedness: had someone made an attempt on the life of Joe Biden or Kamala Harris, the same media would have gone on endlessly about the MAGA threat to national security.

We often hear about the "national divide," but even more obvious is the "Trump divide." For his enthusiasts, Trump and only Trump is the man who can save America at this perilous juncture. In their view, the system—not just the system of government but also our political, civic, and cultural institutions—is the problem, and Trump is the remedy. Trump can do no wrong; Trump himself once said, "I could stand in the middle of Fifth Avenue and shoot somebody, and I wouldn't lost any voters."[9] Trump was obviously exaggerating, but only to make a point. In the sphere of MAGA— the people who want to "make America great again"—Trump is the Teflon Man, the one and only, and now, especially after the assassination attempt, a leader under God's protection. Trump is virtually beyond reproach.

For his critics, by contrast, Trump can do no right. Much worse than that, Trump represents a clear and present danger to American democracy. He is a would-be authoritarian who seeks to extinguish our whole system of government. In addition to establishing a dictatorial regime at home, he would also coddle and befriend foreign dictators like Vladimir Putin. Is it any surprise that people who think and talk like this would not be too terribly disturbed if someone were to take Trump out?

Trump's critics point to Trump's statement that, if re-elected, he might consider being "dictator for a day."[10] They invoke surprisingly positive remarks that Trump has made about Putin, Xi, even Kim Jong Un. They cite Trump's post on Truth Social calling for even the Constitution to be set aside in order to eradicate election fraud.

Trump wrote, "Do you throw the Presidential Election Results of 2020 OUT and declare the RIGHTFUL WINNER, or do you

have a NEW ELECTION? A Massive Fraud of this type and magnitude allows for the termination of all rules, regulations and articles, even those found in the Constitution."[11] Trump, they charge,
is a populist who is not above rousing popular passions against the
lawful institutions of society, thus inspiring—if not directing—the
January 6 invasion and occupation of the US Capitol with a view to
challenging the certification of Joe Biden and Kamala Harris.

For Trump's allies, such "evidence" is ludicrous. Trump was
obviously joking about being a one-day dictator. Well, yes, but is
dictatorship something to joke about? Could it be that Trump was
half-serious? How to explain Trump's seemingly careless disregard
for the Constitution which is the supreme law of the land? And
while there is no evidence Trump called for the breaching of the
Capitol—Trump, on the contrary, called for the protesters to march
"peacefully and patriotically" toward the legislative halls of government—there remains a serious question.

Maybe Trump didn't invite an insurrection, but isn't it true that
he could have? Isn't it true that he still could? Imagine if Trump, in
the middle of one of his criminal trials, declared the whole system
of justice a sham and called upon Americans to rise up and overthrow the corrupt partisan prosecutors, judges and juries hell bent
on locking him up. I don't exactly know what would happen, in
such an instance, but my point is that one man, and only one man,
in America today has that kind of power.

Joe Biden couldn't call for an insurrection. It's not even worth
mentioning Kamala Harris in this context. If any Republican other
than Trump called for an insurrection—imagine Marco Rubio
doing this, or Nikki Haley, or even Ron DeSantis—no one would
show up. In this respect, Trump's supporters who dismiss such possibilities are underestimating their own man, while Trump's adversaries, who raise such fearsome prospects, seem to have a better grasp

of the magnitude of the man. Indeed, they fear him so much that they routinely compare him to Hitler circa 1933. They admit, of course, that he hasn't done any Final Solution—at least not yet—but no one thought Hitler would go to such lengths in the early stages of his rule.

Since Trump's adversaries view him in such extreme terms, they are willing to destroy him "by any means necessary," to use one of their own phrases. What would be out of bounds for Germans to do to stop Hitler at the very beginning? Pretty much, nothing! And so for Democrats, keeping Trump off the ballot isn't an impediment to democracy; it is a means of rescuing democracy. And when Trump still runs, they consider a vote for Trump to be a vote to end democracy and a vote against him to be a vote for saving democracy.

The sheer intensity of this rhetoric is profoundly abnormal. What does it mean to cast a vote to end democracy? Democracy is a system for counting votes to ascertain the will of the people. We vote within a democracy, but we don't vote on whether to have democracy, or whether we want democracy to continue. Strangely, leading Democrats think that Trump's voters somehow want him to discontinue our entire system of government!

Trump is not unusual, of course, in drawing praise and criticism from opposite ends of the political spectrum. Pretty much anyone running for president does that. But conventional politicians typically inspire more moderate reactions, and moreover, the supporters and critics generally agree on the type of man that they are voting for or against. "Bill Clinton might be a womanizer, but he's a good president so I'm voting for him." "I don't care if Bill Clinton has good policies; I don't think someone with his low character ought to be president."

Normally the disagreement over a politician mainly represents disagreement over the issues that the politician stands for. Democrats backed Jimmy Carter because he stood for what they stood for; Republicans opposed him because he opposed their positions on a variety of foreign and domestic issues. Republicans liked George W. Bush because he generally espoused conservative policies; Democrats opposed him because he rejected their progressive stances across the board. Even so, the tone of the critics in both cases stayed within mainstream parameters. But not with Trump.

The only figure I can think of who inspired the same feverishly intense reactions as Trump is Abraham Lincoln. Although originally an outsider—a "Western" man rather than a Northeasterner— Lincoln became a beloved figure in the North, while he was passionately reviled in the South. Even a cultivated figure like Mary Boykin Chesnut portrayed him in her diary as an oaf, a barbarian, a vile opportunist, an aspiring tyrant.[12]

But even with Lincoln, the intense feelings were not about the man. They carried over to the man, but what people on both sides felt most strongly about was slavery—or more precisely, the question of whether slavery should be permitted to go into the new federal territories. With Trump, by contrast, the ferocity of feeling is all about the man. It's not what he stands for; it's who he is.

Consider the small group of people—mostly traditional Republicans, but also some independents and centrist Democrats— who fall outside the two camps that either love Trump or hate him. This small group, which cannot be dismissed—it might prove the "swing vote" in the 2024 election—seeks to take a middle position by saying, "I don't like Trump, but I like his policies." I know people like this, and I hear some variation of this theme a lot.

But it makes no sense to me. Trump's policies are for the most part mainstream conservative policies. Admittedly, Trump has veered away from the neoconservatism of the Bushes in his antipathy to foreign wars. But Reagan was allergic to foreign wars and very reluctant to commit US troops abroad. Even Trump's positions on immigration and trade are well within the Republican mainstream.

Reagan, I believe, would quite likely have supported a wall, or some equivalent obstacle, to shut down the porous border that Democrats have created in order to let millions of illegals into the United States. Republicans are traditionally free traders, yet it is not a denigration of free trade for Trump to demand that other countries take down their tariffs if they want to sell their goods without tariffs in the United States. Trump seeks a free trade level playing field, which would make global trade more, not less, free.

My point is that Trump's policies are, in this sense, pedestrian; it is Trump the man who is unique. The group that dislikes Trump while liking his policies never seems to consider what kind of man is electable in today's environment to implement the kinds of policies that they say they want. These people rarely consider the toxic political environment in which Trump operates in which figures of a more benign disposition would be eaten alive.

Has it gone unnoticed in these precincts that the very nominees of the GOP in times past—Bob Dole, the Bushes, John McCain, Mitt Romney—have become anathema in their own party, and seem utterly unsuited to national leadership in the America we live in now? "We want normalcy," they chant in unison, seemingly unaware that normalcy of the old type is gone and might never return; moreover, how can you get normalcy back without defeating the malign forces that have imposed perversity and abnormality on our culture and our politics?

This brings me to the second Trump enigma. The first one was the enigma of the American people in their strange and intensely opposed reactions to Trump. The second is the enigma of Trump himself. Here is a man who is under supreme duress. He is attacked mercilessly, in and out of office, every single day. He has been twice impeached by a Democratic House of Representatives, although both impeachments failed in the Senate. He has faced lawsuits that have imposed crippling financial penalties on him and his business. He is facing ninety-one criminal charges, and has already been found guilty of thirty-four felonies in a single case. He could spend the rest of his life in prison.

And for what? Quite obviously, the goal of the Democrats and their allies in the media, the intelligence agencies of government, and yes, powerful elements in the judiciary is to prevent Trump from winning a second term as president. If he had foresworn that, if he had retreated from the field, all of it would have gone away— indeed much of it would not have been attempted in the first place.

Trump is a billionaire. He has the exquisite Mar-a-Lago estate, he has hotels and golf properties around the country and the world, he is a celebrity everywhere he goes, he has available to him a life that even a president might envy. So why risk all that? Why risk his very freedom for a thankless job that, one can safely say, would be deluged with controversy from the moment he assumed office for the second time?

It cannot be said that Trump is doing this for the taste of the presidency, because he has already tasted it. He has been president. Been there, done that! So he cannot be pursuing a second go-around in order to savor the power; he has savored it. Perhaps his critics will say he has an insatiable lust for power, but power to what end?

According to Plutarch, it was the mission of Alexander the Great to rule the entire known world. Is Trump a man of comparable ambition? Specifically, does Trump seek power for its own sake, or does he pursue power to accomplish some distinct goal, either for himself or for others? What goal could possibly be more appealing to a man in his late seventies than the goal of enjoying his luxurious life in the company of his dedicated employees, his devoted family, and his exuberant grandchildren?

We need to unravel these enigmas not merely to understand Trump, but also to understand our current situation, indeed to better understand ourselves. Fortunately we can do it in a single stroke. And in this task we have the help of one of the greatest students and practitioners of American politics, a man who is rightly regarded as America's greatest president, Abraham Lincoln.

On January 27, 1838, a young Abraham Lincoln spoke on the topic of "The Perpetuation of Our Political Institutions" to the Young Men's Lyceum of Springfield, Illinois. This has come to be known as Lincoln's Lyceum speech.[13] While it lacks the mature cadence of Lincoln's later addresses—his first and second inaugural, his Gettysburg address—the Lyceum speech is nevertheless prophetic. It diagnoses a malady in Lincoln's day that is also a malady in our own day. Lincoln's main theme is the subversion of law and the danger of the rise of an American dictator or tyrant who would destroy the foundations of our constitutional republic.

Lincoln begins hauntingly by noting that if America were ever to perish, it would be through internal ruin. "Shall we expect some transatlantic military giant to step the Ocean, and crush us at a blow? Never! . . . If destruction be our lot, we must ourselves be its author and finisher. As a nation of freemen, we must live through all time, or die by suicide." In our time, as in Lincoln's, the danger to the survival of our republic is primarily domestic, not foreign. Foreign enemies might exploit domestic travails, but our biggest danger is the enemy at home.

The founders, Lincoln argues, did their job by creating a new society, what they called a novus ordo seclorum, a new order for the ages. It is our job—the job of subsequent generations—to preserve it. Here, I fast forward to what Lincoln said in a special message to Congress in 1861. The challenge, he warned, is "its successful maintenance against a formidable internal attempt to overthrow it."[14] This warning is no less relevant to our own time as it was to Lincoln's.

Back to the Lyceum address. Our system, says Lincoln, is a system of laws—we are a government of laws and not men. And yet, Lincoln warns of a rising trend of disregard for law, what Lincoln calls "mob rule" or the "mobocratic spirit" that is overtaking the land. The underlying issue, of course, is slavery, but Lincoln downplays the issue. He focuses instead on episodes where angry mobs take the law into their own hands, in one case hanging gamblers in Vicksburg, in another the burning of a Black man suspected of murder in St. Louis, in a third, acts of violence against abolitionists in Lincoln's own state of Illinois.

One might expect Lincoln to close here, perhaps with some proposed remedies against angry roving mobs. But Lincoln steers his argument in an unexpected direction. He raises the prospect of an unnamed tyrant coming to power in America who ruthlessly exploits the mobocratic spirit and channels it to his own purposes. Such a figure, Lincoln says, is not merely possible; his ascent should be expected. In fact, Lincoln raises the tantalizing prospect that the unnamed tyrant—the would-be destroyer of the republic—is already here.

Astonishingly Lincoln considers the approach of tyranny in America not from the point of view of the people whose freedom is at stake; he does so from the point of view of the tyrant. Ordinary politicians, he says, might be content with merely upholding the structure the founders put in place. That, and the perks of office, are for them sufficient gratification. But not for the tyrant who will not content himself with such modest ambitions.

"The question then," says Lincoln, "is can that gratification be found in supporting and maintaining an edifice that has been erected by others? Most certainly it cannot. Many great and good men sufficiently qualified for any task they should undertake may ever be found, whose ambition would aspire to nothing beyond a seat in Congress, a gubernatorial or a presidential chair; but such belong not to the family of the lion, or the tribe of the eagle."

Lincoln continues. "What! Think you these places would satisfy an Alexander, a Caesar or a Napoleon? Never! Towering genius disdains a beaten path. It seeks regions hitherto unexplored. It sees no distinction in adding story to story, upon the monument of fame, created to the memory of others. It denies that it is glory enough to serve under any chief. It scorns to tread in the footsteps of any predecessor, however illustrious. It thirsts and burns for distinction; and if possible it will have it, whether at the expense of emancipating slaves, or enslaving freemen."

What is one to make of this astounding prophetic warning from America's wisest and most far-seeing leader? Lincoln ascribes an almost sympathetic motivation to tyrants—they are men of such caliber that they seek distinction above the run of the mill; mere human laws cannot contain them; they blaze their own paths of genius and greatness. Yet Lincoln could not be more clear that we should beware of such people.

So who are they? Is Lincoln referring to the man who would become his chief political rival, the Democrat Stephen Douglas? Did he have in mind the powerful South Carolina Senator John C. Calhoun, avid champion of slavery as a "positive good"? Lincoln docs not specifically say. The speech as a whole defies easy application, especially across the distance of nearly two centuries, and yet Trump's critics have triumphantly invoked it to say, here we go, Lincoln was obviously warning about the rise of a tyrannical menace like Donald Trump.

Here's Never Trump columnist Bret Stephens, writing in the *New York Times*. According to Stephens, "Lincoln knew in 1838" what America would face in our own time. Trump and his allies represent, in Stephens' words, "men in the mold of Caesar or Napoleon who would sooner tear down than defend republican institutions in order to slake a thirst for glory." Writing in *The Guardian*, Jason Wilson invokes the specter of "Red Caesarism" to describe the ascent of Trump and his Make America Great Again movement. Such people, columnist Damon Linker insists, "are waiting in the wings to impose a dictatorship on the United States."[15]

The focus on Caesar, rather than Napoleon and Alexander, seems appropriate. Napoleon and Alexander relied on foreign conquests to consolidate their power. Caesar, however, was suspected of subverting the Roman republic from within. He rose from the aristocracy to then ally with the masses against the aristocrats and Roman elites. The people, just as much as his military conquests, were the source of his power. With mobs baying in the streets, Caesar could govern as an emperor in all but name.

But before we consider the application of Lincoln's speech to our own time, let's return to the question of whom Lincoln had in mind when he invoked the prospect of an American Caesar. Who specifically was he warning against? Let's go back to Lincoln's ominous description. An American Caesar, he says, would not hesitate to pursue distinction "whether at the expense of emancipating slaves or enslaving freemen." In other words, Lincoln here considers the shocking possibility that the Caesar he is warning against is himself!

Here we come to the central argument that I want to pursue in this book. Trump, like Lincoln, faces a problem of widespread lawlessness in society. In Trump's case the lawlessness comes from illegals crossing the border by the millions, from crime that goes unprosecuted and unpunished, from riots that are encouraged by political authorities and the media, and from the conduct of police agencies of government that operate like "thugs with badges."

Trump's critics insist that the lawlessness is coming from him. I'll explore that charge, but only to expose how baseless it is. Lincoln, too, endured the accusation that he was the source of lawlessness. Just like Trump, Lincoln was charged with being a dictator and a tyrant, not only by Democrats in his own time, but also by some historians and commentators right up to our own day.

Lincoln, like Trump, was a larger-than-life figure. He too had Caesarian dimensions, and as we see from the Lyceum speech, he recognized the Caesarian temptation, even in himself. Did he succumb to it? Early in the Civil War, Lincoln suspended habeas corpus, which is a core protection of constitutional rights. Quite clearly the Constitution gives Congress—not the President—the power to suspend habeas corpus in the event of a national emergency.

But Lincoln argued that the outbreak of the war had prevented Congress from being able to safely convene. Congress simply could not exercise its constitutional power. And so Lincoln was compelled to do it on Congress's behalf. When Congress later could meet, Lincoln explained, they did in fact ratify his exercise of that authority.

So Lincoln denied that he was acting unconstitutionally, even though a case can be made that he was. What I find most interesting is what Lincoln says next. "Are all the laws but one to go unexecuted, and the Government itself go to pieces lest that one be violated?" In other words, should the "Government be overthrown when it was believed that disregarding the single law would tend to preserve it?"[16]

Here Lincoln makes the striking point that even if he had violated the Constitution it would be worth doing if the country's survival was itself at stake. In other words, the Constitution exists for the people, and not the other way around. It makes no sense to cling to habeas corpus and watch the entire ship of state go down, in which case no rights—including that one—could be protected. I agree with Lincoln here, and it is in this context that I understand Trump's statement that the problem of widespread election fraud must be corrected even if the Constitution itself needs to be set aside in doing so.

Maybe the Constitution does not specifically anticipate the kind of subversion of electoral democracy that is going on now. Consequently it is in the interest of the Constitution, and the system of government it helped create, to address that issue frontally and without regard to constitutional silences and ambiguities that are inadequate to the task at hand. Even if taken literally, Trump's view of the Constitution here is quite consistent with what Lincoln argued in the habeas corpus case. Trump, like Lincoln, is attempting to save and not subvert our system of government.

There is subversion—the threat of tyranny is real enough—but it comes from the other side. The Democrats today have established a tyrannical regime that not only condones lawlessness on the street, but also incorporates lawlessness into the institutions of government. Unlike Caesar, the Democrats don't ally with the people against the elites; rather, they are elites who carry out their schemes against the people in the name of the people. They say they are "saving democracy." In this way they resemble virtually all modern tyrannies that undermine law and democracy while pretending to march behind the very banners of law and democracy.

When there is a contest between elites and the people, it is important to recognize that there is a danger of tyranny from either side. In the English civil war, tyranny was clearly represented by the rule of the king, Charles I. But when Charles was overthrown and subsequently executed, Oliver Cromwell, acting in the name of parliament, established a regime no less tyrannical and indifferent to the rights and welfare of the people. Cromwell proved no less autocratic than the monarch whom he replaced.

The American founders, who were students of English history, knew this. They understood, one might say, the problem of the wolf and the sheep. Lincoln himself, in an 1864 address at a Baltimore fair, expressed the problem perfectly. "We all declare for liberty but in using the same word we do not all mean the same thing. The shepherd drives the wolf from the sheep's throat, for which the sheep thanks the shepherd as a liberator, while the wolf denounces him for the same act as the destroyer of liberty. Plainly the sheep and the wolf are not agreed upon a definition of the word liberty."[17]

Lincoln is being slightly whimsical here, but he captures the irony that the wolf, no less than the sheep, appeals to liberty. The tyrannical regimes of today insist that their actions are expressions of the highest regard for liberty. Lincoln contrasts the actions of the wolf, whose real concern is only for himself, with those of the shepherd, whose concern is with protecting the sheep from the wolf. The shepherd differs from the wolf, not because he lacks the power to harm the sheep, but because he chooses to care for them and protect them.

Shepherds, however, cannot protect the sheep in their care if they are not stronger than the wolves that seek to prey on them. To put it bluntly, it takes a Caesar to defeat a Caesar! This is the subtle message of the Lyceum address. Lincoln fully understood that the crisis of 1860 required a leader of titanic ambition and capability to meet the grave threat posed by the powerful forces of lawlessness and sedition. So too, I argue, Trump is the eight-hundred-pound gorilla who understands his own titanic powers, and is ready to deploy them against the formidable forces of evil and tyranny in our society.

Of course, Lincoln's analogy of the shepherd and the wolf can be challenged with a Machiavellian objection. Isn't the shepherd a disguised wolf? Isn't the shepherd protecting the sheep only to ready them for the slaughter? Isn't the shepherd, no less than the wolf, doing what he does with an eye to his dinner? Lincoln's answer is that he is invoking the shepherd of the Bible, the shepherd of the psalms and the Book of Isaiah and also the New Testament, in which Jesus is likened to a good shepherd.

In analyzing the Lyceum address, political scientist Harry Jaffa makes the point that "the strength of the wolf inspires terror, yet there is nothing wonderful about it because it is joined to the wolf's predatory nature." The wolf is selfish, but so, after all, are the sheep. But the good shepherd is a mystery, because while he has the power to destroy the sheep, he chooses to protect them. Jaffa argues that "it is the contrast between the shepherd's gentleness and his strength, and the mystery of why he denies himself human or selfish gratification, that arouses wonder."

The only explanation for the shepherd's behavior is that he loves the sheep and therefore acts to promote their welfare, rather than his own. Ultimately, Jaffa concludes, Lincoln answered for his actions not to the Constitution or even to the American people but rather to that higher voice heard only by himself, "Well done thou good and faithful servant."[18] Trump, like Lincoln, is what Aristotle called the great-souled man, the man who is moved not by ordinary selfish ambitions but with a greater regard for noble and redeeming actions that the situation demands of him.

Here, I believe, is the resolution of the two enigmas I outlined at the beginning of this chapter. The Left calls Trump a tyrant because they recognize in him colossal and titanic power. He could be a Caesar if he wanted to. And so the Left accuses him of being a Caesar, even though Trump has never acted like a Caesar, and deep down they know he is not a Caesar. What they really fear is his power and his burning passion for the country's founding ideals.

He represents a threat—the only serious threat—to their Caesarian project. Tyranny can never be consolidated in America while there are men like Trump to stop it. The Left hates Trump for the same reason that wolves hate good shepherds.

Trump's own supporters recognize Trump's power, and also the gentleness that is contained within that power. Trump has the power to do harm, but he has no intention to use that power, because he loves his country and he loves its people and he seeks to protect in the manner of Lincoln's shepherd. Trump's MAGA enthusiasts "get" him, and they are loyal to him because he is loyal to them.

Ironically, there are some Republicans who are made uncomfortable by Trump's dimensions—by his power—for the simple reason that they don't possess it. It bewilders them. They would rather be led by a sheep than a shepherd, someone more like, well, themselves. So they are constantly wishing that Trump accommodate himself to their petty demands: stay with the herd, stop seeking out the wolf, be more civil to the wolf, live and let live, stop making such aggressive noises toward the wolf. These Republicans make a virtue out of cowardice and weakness, and their highest aspiration is to be the sheep that is eaten last. They refuse the assistance of the shepherd "on principle."

Having resolved the first enigma, I now turn to the second, and by recalling it you can see that we already have the answer to it. Why, after all, does Trump do it? The reason is because his motivation is not selfish but unselfish. He has nothing personally to gain from another term in office. It promises him unceasing turmoil, conflict, aggravation. The tyrannical Left, after all, will not go down without a vicious fight. Wolves don't surrender; you have to subdue them and chase them away.

Yet Trump persists because he knows that his country and its people need him. He is the sole leader on our side who has the power of Caesar but the aspiration to save the country from the Caesarian threat. We don't need to remake Trump or tame him or curb him or change him in any way; Trump "as is" is what we need and pretty much all we need. Our job is to get behind him and work with him to defeat the evil forces that are working overtime to destroy this country.

CHAPTER 2

THE MAKING OF A COLOSSUS

Why, man, he doth bestride the narrow world like a Colossus.[19]
—William Shakespeare, *Julius Caesar*

In the above quotation, Cassius describes Caesar as a "colossus," which is to say a person larger than life, a giant. Cassius says that compared to Caesar the other Romans are "petty men" who "walk under his huge legs" and "peep about to find ourselves dishonorable graves." In other words, Caesar is so grand that he just makes everyone else look bad. And through the centuries, of course, the term Caesar, with its variations like Kaiser and Czar, will become the title for a supreme leader, not just a king but a sort of king of kings.

Especially now after the failed assassination attempt, Trump has reached iconic or even mythic status. He is a kind of Caesar in stature, even if he does not aspire to rule dictatorially like Caesar. The question is how Trump became that way. This is the story of the making, or perhaps I should say self-making, of Donald Trump. I use the term self-making because Trump is very much the architect of his own destiny. He has built his own ladder; he is indebted to himself for himself. I will try, in this and subsequent chapters, to capture the heroism of that achievement.

Ironically, the unceasing venom of the Left shows that they know he's a colossus. They need a whole army to take him down. One indictment will not suffice, as it would have sufficed for any other Republican; they need ninety-one. One conviction will not do, not even if it incorporates thirty-four felonies; they need multiple convictions, and maybe that won't be enough. Every institution from academia to the media to Hollywood to the intelligence agencies of government, not to mention the entire establishment political class, including Never Trump Republicans, is mobilized against Trump. Still, they have not succeeded in vanquishing this man who still looms large over them.

By and large, mainstream Republicans, and certainly the GOP establishment, simply do not recognize Trump's power. Only the MAGA rank and file does. So often do I hear from Republican establishment types, "I'm voting for Trump because I like his policies." This is said in a rueful, grudging tone of voice. Here's my reaction: Yeah, but you have the same policies and you're not Trump. The Left expends no energy taking you down. You inspire no fear in them, or in anyone. No one accuses you of being a dictator, and even if you said you wanted to, everyone would laugh.

Even some of Trump's ardent supporters understate, and underestimate, his uniqueness. "We want Trump because we need a businessman." Yet most businessmen couldn't run the country. Even if they could, they couldn't get elected. The piranhas would eat them alive. "Trump's great virtue is that he is an outsider." Again, most outsiders would have no clue about how to make their way into the deepest corridors of power. Even if by some miracle, they got there, they would have no idea what to do once they arrived. It's no surprise that the last "outsider" to reach the presidency before Trump was Eisenhower, and he was the supreme commander of the Allied Forces in World War II.

We heard the same kind of nonsense a generation ago about Reagan. "He's such a good leader because he used to be an actor." What? Let's make a list of prominent actors from that era: Ed Asner, Alan Alda, Sylvester Stallone, Bette Midler. Regardless of their politics, could any of these actors become a highly successful president, win two terms, and revive the economy and the American sprit? Absolutely not.

Trump, likewise, became an entrepreneurial titan and a major cultural celebrity before he set foot into politics. He built one of the largest brands in the world, akin to Coke or Pepsi. Actually, he's bigger than Coke and Pepsi put together. What does it take to do these things simultaneously? There are lots of wealthy people in our society, but very few of them are famous. (Fame is much more rare than money.) We only recognize the names of a handful of them. Even when we do, their fame is confined to a particular niche. Trump, however, is in a league of his own.

I want to show in this chapter how Trump became Trump, a transformation and self-creation that preceded his meteoric rise in politics. I'll highlight Trump's two landmark "crossings," his crossing of the bridge into Manhattan, and his coming down the escalator at Trump Tower to declare his candidacy for President. I'll also show the emergence of Trump's signature personality, emphasizing how he relates so well to ordinary people and also his entertaining and distinctively pungent sense of humor—key traits of a populist icon.

Trump himself tells the key elements of his entrepreneurial story in his book *The Art of the Deal*. "I didn't want," he writes, "to be in the business my father was in." A strange thing to say, since his father was in real estate! But Fred Trump made his money through rent-controlled and rent-stabilized housing units in Queens and Brooklyn. A cautious, self-effacing man, quite unlike his son,

Fred Trump liked to say that collecting rent was the ideal way to make money. Donald Trump—who was not his father's son in this respect—disagreed.

Trump wanted to cross the bridge and do business in Manhattan, and collecting small rents could not have been further from his mind. "I was looking to make a statement—something worth a big effort. . . . What attracted me was the challenge of building a spectacular development on almost one hundred acres by the river on the West Side of Manhattan, or creating a huge new hotel next to Grand Central Station at Park Avenue and Forty Second Street."[20]

In a remarkable, little-known book, *The Entrepreneur*, the economist Joseph Schumpeter says the defining feature of the entrepreneur is "the dream and desire to found a private kingdom." In fact, the secret aspiration of the entrepreneur is to found a "dynasty," to project the dream beyond his own life. It is, Schumpeter admits, "the nearest approach to medieval lordship possible to modern man." The entrepreneur's motivation, Schumpeter writes, is not primarily monetary success. Rather, it is "the will to conquer, the impulse to fight, to prove oneself superior to others, to succeed for the sake, not of the fruits of success, but of success itself." Schumpeter likens it to sport. "The financial result is a secondary consideration, or at all events, mainly valued as an index of success and a symptom of victory." It is entirely subordinate to "the joy of creating, of getting things done, or simply of exercising one's energy and ingenuity."[21] And Trump says the same, if not in the same words.

Early in his career, Trump set his sights on the Commodore Hotel—built in 1919 and named after "Commodore" Cornelius Vanderbilt. Yet in the depressed real estate market of the 1970s, this historic property had become a sorry sight. The brick façade was filthy, the lobby dingy, and derelicts reclined in the hallways.

Management didn't mind; no one wanted to stay at the Commodore, despite paltry room rates.

"But as I approached the hotel," Trump writes, "something completely different caught my eye. It was about nine in the morning and there were thousands of well-dressed Connecticut and Westchester commuters flooding onto the streets from Grand Central Terminal and the subway stations below." Here we have a critical scene. A progressive critic might interpret it by noting the ironic contrast between the upbeat commuters and the depressed Commodore. Once the hotel was historic, but now history had passed it by.

Trump's interpretation was more prosaic: there's a business opportunity here. "What I saw was a superb location." Affluent prospects were passing through it every day. "The problem was the hotel, not the neighborhood." So Trump got the crazy idea to buy the Commodore. He was a brash kid who just came across the bridge from Queens. But he did the first thing entrepreneurs do: he came up with a big new idea for a venture. Schumpeter calls this a "combination," by which he means a new product, a new landscape, a new way of doing things or a new way of living.

It's one thing to have an idea, of course, and quite another to figure out how to do it. Trump didn't have the money to buy the Commodore. Neither was Daddy much help. "I went to my father and told him I had a chance to make this deal for this huge midtown hotel. He refused to believe I was serious." Trump had to figure out how to buy it and how to run it, even though he lacked the funds to buy it or to renovate it, and he had no experience in operating an upscale Manhattan hotel.

Trump negotiated a bargain price with the owners, who were eager to sell but had to be convinced Trump could afford to buy. Trump convinced them to sign a paper listing the terms. Then

Trump went to banks and told them the owners of the Commodore
had consented to sell to him, so if the banks loaned him the asking
price, plus the money to upgrade the hotel, he could put up the
Commodore itself as collateral. It was, as Trump himself admits, a
"juggling act." But the banks went for it and the seller came through,
so Trump got the Commodore.

Taking it on was a huge risk. Many academics portray risk, and
willingness to take risk, as the defining feature of an entrepreneur.
But Trump confesses he hates risk. "People think I'm a gambler. I've
never gambled in my life. It's been said I believe in the power of positive thinking. In fact, I believe in the power of negative thinking. I
always go into the deal anticipating the worst."

Trump's creative stroke was to re-imagine the Commodore, to
remake it in his own image. He intended "to cover the brick façade
with an entirely new curtain wall of highly reflective glass." Trump's
plan drew fire from city planners, architectural critics, and media
pundits. This was friendly fire; Trump was not in the political arena,
so he didn't get the unrelentingly savage opposition he gets now.
The critics groused that Trump was violating the architectural norm
of the area, breaking away from the classical look of Grand Central
Station and ornamented brick-and-limestone building along the
block.

Trump had a different idea. The point of the reflective glass, he
felt, was to make the hotel a kind of mirror of the spectacular landscape of New York City itself. "By choosing this highly reflective
glass, I've created four walls of mirrors. Now when you go across
Forty Second Street or go over the Park Avenue ramp, you see the
reflection of Grand Central Terminal, the Chrysler Building, and all
the other landmarks, which otherwise you might not have noticed
at all."

What we see here is Trump's genius for spectacle, his acumen for salesmanship. Trump has shown this marketing flair throughout his career, and it carries over into politics. When he built Trump Tower, he pitched it as the most desirable place to live in New York. "We were selling fantasy," he admits. His business team informed him that a competing property—Museum Tower—had lowered its prices. They told Trump, "We're in trouble."

Here's how Trump reacted. "I thought for a minute, and I realized that actually the opposite was true. Museum Tower had done itself damage. The sort of wealthy people we were competing for don't look for bargains in apartments. They may want bargains in everything else, but when it comes to a house, they want the best, not the best buy. By pricing its apartments lower than ours, Museum Tower had just announced that it was not as good as Trump Tower."[22]

Finally, Trump solved the problem of how to operate the Commodore. He partnered with the Hyatt hotel chain to do it. At first, Trump's people advised him against splitting the profits 50-50 with Hyatt. Hyatt wanted to rename the Commodore the Grand Hyatt, and Trump agreed. The reason was that, in Hyatt, Trump had found a partner experienced in running hotels and willing to share the financial risk by reimbursing Trump a significant portion of the funds expended to acquire and upgrade the Commodore.

And it paid off for him. The Commodore reopened as the Grand Hyatt, it was successful, and Trump and Hyatt split the profits. Eventually, a dispute arose between the two parties, which they settled in a conventional business way: In 1996, Hyatt gained complete ownership by buying out Trump's half-share in the hotel for $142 million. Today, decades later, the Trump Organization has the experience, and doesn't have to go to Hyatt; they operate their own hotels, resorts, and casinos across America and in foreign locations. But the Commodore gave Trump his big start, and that's why I've focused on telling that story.

Trump's real estate career is by no means one of unalloyed business success. In Trump's book *The Art of the Comeback*, he describes
seeing a homeless man holding a begging cup on the street. This was
in the early 1990s, and two of Trump's big properties—the Trump
Taj Mahal and the Trump Plaza Hotel—had just gone bankrupt.
Trump owed $900 million. Pointing to the homeless man, Trump
remarked "He's a beggar, but he's worth $900 million more than
me."[23]

Reviewing this passage in the book, Dylan Matthews, a writer
for the website Vox, reacts with revulsion to Trump's casual, almost
jovial, attitude here. "You'd think this kind of story would result in
some kind of self-reflection," Matthews writes. But in Trump's case,
"Nah." Trump seems "uninterested in his failure."[24] In progressive
academic and journalistic precincts, self-reflection is what you do
when things take a downward turn. Failure is an occasion for some
high-toned navel-gazing, asking whether your busts and bankruptcies are a real measure of your worth as a person.

To such people, Trump's willingness to forge boldly ahead
seems downright surreal. The man must be demented! Total lack
of introspection! Yet Trump weathered the storm and went on to
massively successful new ventures. These early struggles demonstrate
his toughness and bravery, and also equipped him for the greater
toughness and bravery he would need in the political sphere.

Trump himself discussed how crucial these early hardships were
to his strength as a survivor. Here's an excerpt from his conversation
with Charlie Rose in 1992.

Rose: What is the most important thing to a guy like you?
Trump: I think the way I've survived, the quality in which I've lived
under the survival mode, the image that I've portrayed during this survival period...Some tough, smart people gave up. They just gave up.

They said, I can't do it anymore. I think the way in which I survived
was very important to me.[25]

Trump survived. Eventually the New York real estate market revived,
and he recovered his lost fortune, and then some. Not that there
wouldn't be reversals in the future. He won some and he lost some,
but he won more than he lost, and he's got a vastly bigger brand, and a
vastly bigger bank account, than all his critics put together.

While maintaining his business empire through the years, Trump
also managed to convert his entrepreneurial success into cultural
celebrity. This turned out to be critical for his subsequent political
ascent. Think of how Trump impressed himself on the American
imagination with his trademark "You're fired" from his role in the
hit television show *The Apprentice*. That alone solidified Trump's
image as a tough, no-nonsense business guy. Trump's persona was
that of a guy who could make the hard decisions.

Somehow, over time, Trump was everywhere, from being interviewed on the talk shows like Charlie Rose, Ellen DeGeneres, and
Oprah Winfrey to cameo roles in movies like *Home Alone 2* to
guest-hosting on *Saturday Night Live*. Madame Tussaud museums
had wax sculptures of Trump. He was regularly satirized by Garry
Trudeau in the *Doonesbury* comic strip. Rappers sang about his
wealth and lifestyle, making him the embodiment of urban aspiration and worldly success. Trump was featured in video games. He
was seen in the company of promoter Don King at the big boxing
fights. Since the late 1980s, he was involved in WWE program-
ming, which is professional wrestling.

Some of this, of course, stemmed from his ownership of hotels
and casinos which feature boxing and other forms of entertainment.
Tellingly, in Trump's movie roles he always played himself. In other
words, he was already seen as a larger-than-life movie "character"

and he didn't have to play a fictional one. But Trump's cultural celebrity requires a wider explanation. What made Trump so savvy about popular culture?

Specifically, how did he develop his distinctive way of talking and relating to people which connected with the worlds of sports and entertainment? How did a billionaire like him reach people far removed from his own orbit of fame and success? These questions are closely connected to my Caesar analogy, because Caesar's genius was to mobilize the people against the aristocrats in the Roman Senate. How did he do it? Military prowess. Caesar went from conquest to conquest and the people went nuts. Trump, obviously, must do it a different way. So what is that way?

I have three answers to that question. Trump, although a business and cultural mogul, developed a natural style of relating to ordinary people. Second, in a manner that his political critics despise and his supporters love, Trump is a natural comedian and entertainer. Third, Trump is, even in small matters, ruthlessly honest, and while this rubs some people the wrong way, it is also a powerful source of his broad-based appeal. So let's see how he cultivated, and even in his early career demonstrated, these qualities.

Trump is a New Yorker—one might say a New Yorker's New Yorker—which is to say he is brash, overstated, and a bit of a know-it-all. Talk to any doorman in New York City and they expostulate on a range of issues as if they were noted experts on topics ranging from finance to food to world travel to politics. Another way to put it is that every doorman working a high-rise apartment building or hotel in New York is a little Trump.

Moreover, Trump embraces popular culture and has cultivated a lifestyle that ordinary people can identify with, if not imitate. I know a handful of billionaires, and quite a lot of rich people, and most of them—even the ones that started out poor—have seceded from the middle class. This is the distinguishing mark of their affluence. They eat in fine restaurants, they travel to exotic places, they cultivate elite hobbies and interests, such as trying to get themselves, or their wives, on the opera or museum board. They seek the approval of other affluent people, and they crave trophies of social recognition, like honorary degrees from elite universities.

Trump has all that—he graduated from Wharton Business School, he owns golf courses patronized by the rich and famous, he has a magnificent collection of art and architecture. At the same time, Trump lives in the manner of a poor man's fantasy of a rich man. Some wealthy people deride him for this, as if Trump were not "really" rich, even though he's much richer than they are.

Yet these scoffers are right that Trump is a guy who eats burgers and fries, and drinks Coke and diet Coke. He's not into showing off his Picasso sketches and paintings, like some other people I know. He likes gold and gold-plated things. He likes to see his name in lights. He likes famous people, and he likes beautiful models. He prefers to own the Miss Universe pageant to being chairman of the Boston Symphony Orchestra. He measures success, his own as well as the success of others, in terms of ratings and sports scores and the amount of money in the bank.

If you're a white guy from Pulaski, a Latino from the Rio Grande Valley, or a Black guy from the Bronx, you probably think, "If I ever got rich, I'd like to have a home with thirty-five bedrooms. I'd probably go for gold-gilded chairs and curtains and tapestries. I'd like to have people fly in my private jet and eat burgers and fries. I'd like to be seen in the company of Miss Venezuela or Miss France." In short, there are a whole lot of people who wouldn't mind living like Donald Trump, or even being Donald Trump.

This explains how Trump, albeit a billionaire, connects with ordinary people—they share the same aspirations, with the only difference being that Trump has gotten there and they haven't. The reason rappers were drawn to Trump is that he embodied liberation from the drudgery of poverty, hardship, and want into the promised land of abundance, beauty, power, and success.

They also recognized him as one of their own, and this brings me to a neglected key to Trump's cultural celebrity, namely, his distinctive manner of speaking and writing. Trump has a working-class manner of talking that is blunt, down-to-earth, and even vulgar in the original meaning of the term—which means common. Poor and lower middle-class people of all races recognize this and identify with it.

I asked Lara Trump about this, in our interview for the movie, and she said Trump spent his life talking to construction workers at the various job sites; he learned to speak their language so that he could relate to them. Ditto with the people who worked in his hotels and casinos and on his golf resorts. Even now, Trump lets slip an occasional "bullshit" or "sonsofbitches" and it takes the political world by surprise, not because those people don't talk like that, but because they don't talk like that publicly. Trump rejects the proprieties of the poseur class.

This is not to say that Trump is simply a working class guy who made it big. Not at all. Most working class guys, for all their bravado, are pretty inarticulate about the cosmopolitan spheres of culture and politics. They talk big while you're waiting to get your car, but if you put them on a talk show, they wouldn't know what to say. Their social media, if they have one, bears no resemblance whatever to Trump's Twitter account or his Truth Social. One may say that Trump is a sort of literary musician and they are not. Rappers, who are themselves literary musicians of a sort, get this about Trump.

Trump is also a comedian and an entertainer. His one-liners have a mark of genius, and he showed that even before he climbed into the political arena. Let's look at a sample of Trump's early comments from media interviews and from his social media posts. Here are a representative sample of them, with my accompanying commentary in parentheses.

I had some beautiful pictures taken in which I had a big smile on my face. I looked happy, I looked content, I looked like a very nice person, which in theory I am.[26] (My favorite part of this quip is "in theory.")

I think I'm actually humble. I think I'm much more humble than you would understand.[27] (Hilarious. This is straight out of the comedy handbook and in the genre of "My greatest virtue is my modesty.")

I'm intelligent. Some people would say I'm very, very, very intelligent.[28] (Trump loves to preface his extravagances with "some people would say," as if he were merely—and objectively—referencing public opinion.)

While Bette Midler is an extremely unattractive woman, I refuse to say that because I always insist on being politically correct.[29] (There's a name for this figure of speech, Apophasis, in which you insult someone while disclaiming you are doing it. Sample usage: "I reject ad hominem attacks, so I'm not going to mention your two bankruptcies, the fact that your wife left you, and your porn addiction.")

Arianna Huffington @ariannahuff is unattractive both inside and out. I fully understand why her former husband left her for a man—he made a good decision.[30] (Arianna Huffington is the founder of the Huffington Post.)

Viagra is wonderful, if you need it. I've just never needed it. Frankly, I wouldn't mind if there were an anti-Viagra, something with the opposite effect. I'm not bragging. I'm just lucky, I don't need it.[31] (He doesn't need Viagra, he might even need anti-Viagra, but of course he's "not bragging." Classic.)

The worst thing a man can do is go bald. Never let yourself go bald.[32] (The amusing implication is that baldness is a matter of choice)

Show me someone without an ego, and I'll show you a real loser.[33] (The punchline is a surprise. Generally not having an ego is considered a positive trait. Trump turns it around, while suggesting that successful people are generally people who think highly of themselves. Seeing themselves as highly capable, they go on to prove themselves to be that way.)

What is it about me that gets Larry King his highest ratings?[34] (Instead of asking, "Am I the reason why Larry King gets such high ratings?" Trump assumes that is the case and jumps to the next question, "What is it about me" that produces this result? We are invited to consider which of Trump's innumerable qualities deserve credit and recognition here.)

What I get out of all this is that Trump has a lively curiosity about the intricacies of popular culture. He addresses people, and issues, with a candor that borders on the ruthless. He is always entertaining, not least when he talks about himself. Indeed, he gives himself a large public ego that is not always substantiated by close-up dealings with the man. Debbie and I have both noticed this: Trump in person exudes a modesty and even humility that we found startling, because it contrasted so sharply with his public persona. My conclusion is that his public persona is, at least to some degree, part of his act.

Trump has come to recognize that it's funny to always give himself such high marks. He plays the role like Muhammad Ali, who could get away with saying, "I am the greatest" because he was, in fact, the greatest. Ordinary people recognize and even appreciate the schtick. Trump quite clearly rejects the elite, upper-middle-class nostrum that one should privately harbor a gargantuan ego while making feigned self-deprecating comments about oneself. (Larry David on making a huge fortune by creating *Seinfeld*, "I did okay.")

Thus, when Trump crossed the Rubicon in 2015 by coming down the escalator at Trump Tower and declaring his candidacy for president, he changed not only his own destiny but that of America and also of the world. That was the exact moment that his own world changed—he went from cultural royalty to pariah. He brought out a paroxysm of outrage and resistance of a kind not seen in American politics since Lincoln. You could feel the cultural Left's sense of betrayal: he had been one of them. They were determined to destroy him, not realizing that he was a colossus and they were not, and that in the end they might end up destroying not Trump, but rather themselves.

CHAPTER 3

WHO'S THE REAL DICTATOR?

Towering genius disdains a beaten path. It thirsts and burns for distinction, and if possible, it will have it, whether at the expense of emancipating slaves, or enslaving freemen.[35]

— Abraham Lincoln, Lyceum Speech

In the previous chapter we saw how Trump developed, and displayed, the entrepreneurial prowess and cultural magnetism that prepared him for his entry into the world of politics. That was the moment things changed dramatically for him. Suddenly, he went from cultural royalty to pariah. Immediately he was denounced as a would-be tyrant and a danger to democracy, and the Hitler analogies were all over the media. Trump's great political sin, it seems, was not his entry into politics but his entry into politics as a Republican.

Still, this hardly explains why Trump's critics would call him an autocrat and liken him to the despised autocrats of the twentieth century, from Mussolini to Hitler. Reagan and Bush were despised by Democrats, but they were not generally portrayed as threats to democracy. Nor have these accusations gone away, or subsided in the slightest. If anything, they are more intense now than eight years ago. Trump, we are routinely assured by Democratic officials and leftist media pundits on CNN and MSNBC, will inaugurate an unthinkable regime of autocracy and repression if he is elected in 2024.

I find it interesting that in Shakespeare's play Caesar is viewed by both Cassius and Brutus as a tyrant—this becomes the justification for assassinating him—and yet we never see him do anything tyrannical. Cassius, Brutus and the other conspirators speak darkly about what Caesar might do or will do. Here's Flavius:

> These growing feathers plucked from Caesar's wing
> Will make him fly an ordinary pitch,
> Who else would soar above the view of men
> And keep us all in servile fearfulness.[36]

In other words, we have to cut him down because of what he might do to us. And Brutus takes the same approach.

> He would be crowned:
> How that might change his nature, there's the question.
> It is the bright day that brings forth the adder,
> And that craves weary walking.[37]

Caesar might change and become a snake, so we might as well treat him like a snake and cut his head off! But of course the underlying premise is that Caesar has the overweening ambition to be a tyrant, and if he has the power, he will be. This is precisely what the Democrats and their media allies say about Trump. So in this chapter we confront head-on the question of whether Trump has these tyrannical ambitions, and if not, why are his critics so insistent that he does?

It is one thing to say that Trump will do this, and will do that, if we had not already had Trump in office to see what he did in fact do. Trump's critics latch on to his phrases like "dictator for a day,"

which are quite obviously intended jokingly, or at least half-jok-
ingly, and they say: Aha! He even admits he's going to be like Hitler.
But Hitler proceeded, almost immediately upon his assumption of
power in 1933, to institute a widespread regime of repression. Hitler
didn't govern in a normal way for a term, and then somehow meta-
morphose into a dictator the second time around.

So the premise of this chapter is that actions speak louder than
words, and we can make a sound judgment about Trump by considering his conduct from the time he entered politics to the end of
his first term in office. Here we'll see that Trump displayed all the
largeness and audacity and even pugnaciousness of Caesar, but he
didn't do anything tyrannical—indeed by objective measures he did
the country a lot of good.

Let me put it another way. If Trump were a dictator while he was
President, then he was the most incompetent dictator in the history
of the world. Dictators control the police agencies of government;
Trump was relentlessly pursued by them. He didn't run the agencies;
he spent much of the time running away from them. Moreover, dictators don't lose elections because they control them and rig them in
their favor. Is it conceivable that the Chinese Communists are voted
out of power in China? That the mullahs in Iran lose an election?
Tyrants ensure they stay in power. They certainly never relinquish
power voluntarily; typically, they have to be ousted by force. None
of this applies to Trump.

Even so, none of his critics admitted they were wrong; indeed
they doubled down on him. These are the people—very powerful
people in Congress, in the intelligence agencies, and in the media—
who treated Trump a menace, like an illegitimate president, even
like a traitor. Since traitors are normally hanged or shot, I call this
attempt to frame Trump as a Russian asset the "political assassination" attempt. It was also, of course, a character assassination. Later

in the book we'll examine the ongoing "legal assassination" attempt, and of course the actual assassination attempt—all part of a large and ominous scheme to get rid of Trump "by any means necessary."

Let's begin with the self-confidence with which Trump entered the political fray. Although he was an outsider who had never run for office—it takes supreme confidence to go from running for nothing to running for the presidency—Trump acted from the outset like he was the Republican front-runner, indeed that the other candidates were a kind of nuisance opposition that would soon be swept aside, as indeed they were.

Where did Trump get this self-assurance that could also be interpreted as arrogance? Listen to Trump's exchange with Charlie Rose, going all the way back to 1992. Rose is talking about Trump's bankruptcies and his major slump when he was hugely in debt with no prospect of recovering from it.

> Rose: Did you ever think you'd lose?
> Trump: No.
> Rose: Did you ever lose confidence? Did you ever say…
> Trump: No.
> Rose: "I may not get out of this."
> Trump: No.
> Rose: Not once?
> Trump: Not once.[38]

Quite obviously a man who thinks like this is a Very Scary Guy. He doesn't even consider the possibility of defeat. So Trump entered the political field with a seriousness, a determination, that seemed almost unique in modern American politics. Even Reagan, a man of acknowledged boldness and aplomb, would never say that he "not once" considered the possibility of being knocked down without being able to get up.

Not that Trump was a complete newcomer to politics; he had been commenting on political issues for decades. What is striking to anyone who reviews Trump's early commentary is how consistent it is with what Trump says now. In other words, Trump is the very same man! The difference is that his primary focus then was his business pursuits, and politics seemed a mere extension of that, while now he has turned his business over to his family, and his main focus is politics and "making America great again."

I'm quite amused to see how Trump, starting around 2010, took the same lively and acerbic style of his cultural commentary and imported it into his media interviews and social media posts about politics. Here is a sampling, which once again displays Trump in his characteristic Trumpian mode, pointed, sometimes laugh-out-loud funny, indifferent to norms of political propriety, brazenly honest.

On gay marriage: It's like in golf. A lot of people are switching to these really long putters, very unattractive. It's weird. You see these great players with these really long putters, because they can't sink three-footers anymore. And I hate it. I'm a traditionalist. I have so many fabulous friends who happen to be gay, but I'm a traditionalist.[39]

I hope we never find life on another planet because if we do there's no doubt that the United States will start sending them money.[40]

I think apologizing's a great thing, but you have to be wrong. I will absolutely apologize, sometime in the hopefully distant future, if I'm ever wrong.[41]

On Obama: When I was 18, people called me Donald Trump. When he was 18, @BarackObama was Barry Soweto. Weird.[42]

On John McCain: He's not a war hero. He was a war hero because he was captured. I like people who weren't captured.[43]

On Carly Fiorina: Look at that face! Would anyone vote for that? Can you imagine that, the face of our next president?[44]

If Hillary Clinton can't satisfy her husband, what makes her think she can satisfy America?[45]

I have a Gucci store that's worth more than Romney.[46]

During the Republican primary of 2016, Trump—to everyone's surprise, including mine—made short work of the other candidates, tagging them with his unforgettable nicknames from which none of them were able to easily recover. Jeb Bush became "low energy Jeb" and a "low energy stiff." Ted Cruz was "lyin' Ted." Marco Rubio became "little Marco."

I did not approve, at the time, of Trump strafing his fellow Republicans in this way. Reagan never did it. I was a subscriber to Reagan's so-called Eleventh Commandment, which is "Thou shall not speak ill of a fellow Republican." Because Trump's labels were so unforgettable, his victims never forgot them. But after the primary, Trump proved that he himself was quick to forget and get beyond the acerbities. He worked closely with Ted Cruz on legislation during his term in office, and Cruz and Rubio both gave enthusiastic speeches on Trump's behalf at the 2024 Republican Convention.

Trump, however, persists in being Trump. Along the way to

his presidency, and even subsequently, others who crossed him also got tagged. Jeff Flake became "Jeff Flakey" or simply "Flakey." Bob Corker was "Liddle Bob Corker." John Kasich's failed political record was memorialized in his nickname "1 for 38 John Kasich." Elizabeth Warren, who inflated her native American heritage, was of course "Pocahontas." Journalist Chuck Todd became, on account of his drooping eyelids, "sleepy eyes Chuck Todd."

Of course, Trump's targets and their allies often tried to strike back against Trump by coming up with damaging nicknames for him. But you'll notice that they never really succeeded. Comedian John Oliver thought he could undo Trump if he could convince people to start calling him "Drumpf." This was, as my stepson Justin likes to say, an "epic fail." Others on the Left tried "Orange Man" and "Mango Mussolini" and a few other forgettable labels that are still recycled every now and then, but have long lost their bite.

In recent months, the Left has pretty much given up on trying to outdo Trump in one-liners and verbal repartee where he is the acknowledged Master of the Universe. Instead they write essays on how Trump's humor is itself a sign of his dictatorial tendencies. In March 2024, *Politico* featured "In on the Joke: The Comedic Trick Trump Uses to Normalize His Behavior." The comedic trick, it turns out, is being funny. *Politico* gives a single example that proves the point. Trump is decrying the "dying" steel industry and his attempts to save it, when a woman in the audience let's out an inexplicable, shrill, long-lasting shriek. Without losing a beat, Trump quips, "Wow. She must be in the steel business!" And the audience roars.

Harmless enough, right? But *Politico* warns that Trump's jokes "recast his own liabilities as laughing matters and desensitize his supporters to his most outrageous comments and proposals— the undermining of institutions, the abandonment of allies, mass

deportations, and all but outright invitations for Russian invasions."
Moreover, *Politico* trots out so-called experts in authoritarianism
(itself an amusing concept) to explain that humor is "how autocrats
work" and that Mussolini and Hitler also had a "twisted sense of
humor."[47] (I've watched some Mussolini and Hitler clips, but even
allowing for the content from both men that gets lost in translation,
I seem to have missed the knee-slappers.)

Along the same lines, and around the same time, the *New York
Review* featured Fintan O'Toole's lengthy rumination, "Laugh
Riot," subtitled, "To understand Trump's continuing hold over
his fans, we have to ask: Why do they find him so funny?" The
short answer to this question is because Trump is funny. It would be
funny, for example, to hear Trump riff on Fintan O'Toole's name,
not that Trump would ever bother with such an obscure pedant.

The writer is forced to admit that "Trump is America's biggest
comedian," but seeks to undermine that concession with somber
observations as, "Racist, misogynistic, antisemitic, xenophobic,
anti-disabled and anti-queer jokes have always been used to dehu-
manize those who are being victimized." Moreover, "It creates an
economy of compassion, limiting it to those who are laughing and
excluding those who are being laughed at."[48] In short, hyper-sensitive
leftists cannot appreciate Trump's humor because they are the butts
of most of the jokes.

Back to Trump's sticky nicknames. I think his best one, powerful
for its simplicity and accuracy, was "Crooked Hillary." Hillary has
never gotten over that one, which in part explains her continuing
venom toward Trump. Of course she will never forgive him for narrowly beating her, forever depriving her of a lifelong ambition. In
Trump's words, Hillary was a "nasty horrid woman" who finally got
"schlonged." (In Trumpworld, people don't lose or get defeated; they
get schlonged.) Hillary will never get past how she got "schlonged."

But now I want to make a serious point about how Trump treated Hillary, which goes to the key question of whether Trump conducted himself in the manner of a dictator. Dictators, let's recall, can be counted on to investigate, prosecute, and seek to lock up their political opponents.

During the debates, Trump at one point fired back at her and said, "You'd be in jail." During the presidential campaign, crowds routinely chanted, "Lock her up." And given the way the Clinton Foundation raked in tens of millions of dollars from foreign entities, seemingly in exchange for foreign policy favors doled out by Hillary as Secretary of State, there probably was cause to investigate and indict Hillary once Trump became President and had the power to do so.

But the point is that he didn't do it. He never even directed his Justice Department to investigate Hillary. If anyone suggested it, Trump nixed the idea. Much later, just a couple of months ago, Trump reflected on this. "And they always said, 'Lock her up,' and I felt—and I could have done it but I felt it would have been a terrible thing." Trump said this while noting ironically that he himself was now subject to a range of criminal prosecutions. So the point he was making is that he isn't the one acting like a dictator; the people trying to get him are.[49]

The Democrats brought out two of their biggest guns against Trump, sleazy tactics that have traditionally proven effective against just about every Republican. The first one is the sex scandal. Trump of course had been married thrice, and he was unquestionably a playboy in his early years, and so there was material for his political adversaries to work with. Trump is also given to loose talk, as came out in the infamous *Access Hollywood* tape, which had been recorded in 2005, but was leaked to the *Washington Post* which published it on October 7, a little over a month prior to Election Day.

Trump: "I just start kissing them. It's like a magnet. I don't even wait. When you're a star, they let you do it. You can do anything. Grab them by the pussy." When the tape first came out, my wife Debbie was utterly horrified and said, in her characteristic note of finality, "He's done." I too was not sure how he could recover from this, and it was on the eve of a presidential debate. He would have to justify this inexcusable rhetoric in front of an indignant woman!

But Trump's approach was to pretend like the whole thing was no big deal. He apologized, one of the very few things for which he has ever apologized in his long career, and he dismissed it as locker talk. For insurance—and this shows his political genius—he had several women whom Bill Clinton had sexually assaulted accompany him to the debate. One of them, Juanita Broaddrick, alleged that Clinton forcibly raped her.

Hillary, of course, had notoriously attempted to discredit these women. So Trump's point, without saying a word, was that if Hillary wanted to bring up his loose talk, the women were ready to spring up and talk about her husband's grotesque and possibly criminal actions. Hillary never brought it up. The press continued to lambast Trump for his remarks, but the scandal lost traction, like air going out of a tire. Here Trump proved that a scandal that would have ended the career of any other candidate—certainly any other Republican—had only minimal effect on him.

The other sex scandal involved the porn star Stormy Daniels. Daniels had accused Trump of having sex with her, and she threatened to disclose this in the weeks leading up to the 2016 campaign. She wanted money for her silence. So Trump's lawyer Michael Cohen had arranged a financial payment in exchange for a Non-Disclosure Agreement. The issue isn't whether Trump did it, because rich and powerful people are shaken down this way all the time. It is not uncommon for wealthy individuals or even companies to settle such cases to avoid scandal, even if there is no underlying scandalous conduct.

The issue is that, in paying off Daniels, Trump made it seem like he did it. And so the Left and the Democrats went into high gear, mobilizing their powerful media machine, which as we know is made up of thousands of journalistic apparatchiks, ready to take orders from the Democratic scandal mongers. Stormy Daniels was everywhere, on *60 Minutes*, profiled as a "feminist hero" in the *New York Times*.[50] She even published a book and went on a tour titled *Make America Horny Again*.

The key to the Left's deployment of Daniels is their recognition that conservatives, Republicans, and Christians are straight-laced people. Exploiting virtue, and compelling virtue to take the side of the party of vice—this is what the Stormy Daniels "play" was all about. Daniels, of course, was a pervert. The Left has never minded perversion. If you know anything about the rootless, nomadic life of journalists and political operatives, you'll know that many journalists and operatives are no less perverted than Stormy Daniels. Moreover, virtually no one on the Left has any objection to Stormy Daniels's perversion.

But they know that conservatives do! And Republicans! And Christians! So the strategy is to hurl Daniels in the face of Trump, and then sit back and laugh their heads off, because they know what's going to happen. They've seen it dozens of times before. What's going to happen is that Trump's own side will be outraged. They will not put up with this sleaze. They never have. Thus the Left can count on Trump's own side to knife him over this, and to buy his political carcass.

Yet this time, the strategy that had always worked, that would have worked with any other Republican, didn't work with Trump. Here, in my imaginative rendition, is how it went.

"Hey, Mr. Trump, we've got something for you."

"Oh yeah, what have you got?"

"Stormy Daniels!"

"What else you got?"

Trump's political counter-strategy here is worth spelling out. He acts like it's no big deal. Trump's insight—and this is what Republicans have traditionally missed—is that the whole thing is fake. The Left has no interest in the truth of the matter, and the truth wouldn't matter to them even if they knew it. Rather, they use the charge of "hypocrisy" because they know that only Republicans uphold public moral standards. You cannot accuse Bill Clinton of being a hypocrite because he is pretty much an acknowledged pervert.

So Trump rejects the very premise of the scandal, which he treats as not a scandal at all. He defuses the hypocrisy issue by simply brushing off the charge, not with heated denials, but with a casual, "Who cares?" Essentially, he lowers the moral bar, and then jumps nimbly over it. Throughout, Trump is conveying to the Left, "I see through you. I'm not playing your silly game." And the people who know it's a game, but one that has always worked for them, seethe in rage and loathe him all the more, not for having sex with Stormy Daniels but for outwitting them politically.

The second reliable line of attack against Trump was the Left's insistent accusation that he is a racist. What is the actual basis for this charge? *Vox* tried to spell it out in a 2020 article, "Donald Trump's long history of racism, from the 1970s to 2020." But reading through the list, I could not find a single clear-cut case. Yeah, Trump settled an antidiscrimination case in 1973. So what? Yeah he expressed some doubts in 1993 about a group of Native Americans getting casino rights because "they don't look like Indians to me." They probably weren't.

Yeah, he derided Obama's academic record. "I heard he was a terrible student. How does a bad student go to Columbia and then to Harvard?" This is an accurate observation. The article claims "Trump launched his campaign by calling Mexican immigrants rapists," which is false in that Trump was talking about illegals, not "immigrants," and moreover, he was clear that some of them, not all, were perpetrators of crimes including rape. Entirely true! Finally, *Vox* alleges that "Trump called for a ban on all Muslims coming into the US," even though Trump never said "all Muslims," and in any case the article admits he didn't actually do it.[51]

But the primary exhibit in the *Vox* article, and indeed in all catalogs of Trump's supposed racism, is what Trump said about the Charlottesville "Unite the Right" rally in 2017. Trump has been accused for seven years straight of saying that neo-Nazis and white supremacists, some of whom showed up at that rally, were "fine people." One can locate thousands of media reports that Trump said that. Yet a simple review of the transcript shows that Trump did not say it.

Trump did claim that there were "fine people" on both sides, meaning the side that attended the rally and the side that protested against it. But Trump also said, "And you had people—and I'm not talking about the neo-Nazis and the white nationalists—because they should be condemned totally. But you had many people in that group other than the neo-Nazis and white nationalists."[52]

It should be noted that the media perpetrated this lie about Trump for years knowing it was a lie. Trump consistently lambasted the media during his term in office, sometimes mocking journalists by name. Some people found this ad hominem tiresome, and wished he would cut it out. Reagan never did that; he went above the heads of the media. Reagan was "above the fray," so why should Trump be so "in the fray?"

Because the media, even if biased against Reagan, was not a juggernaut of outright dishonesty and lies, as it became in the Trump era. Trump accurately dubbed them collectively to be "fake news," because he knew there was nothing negative about him, no matter how false or unsubstantiated, that they would not publish, and continue to promulgate even when they knew it was lies. One of Trump's signature feats has been to expose the shameless dishonesty of the mainstream media, not only on the racism issue but across the board.

It took Trump a long time—several years—to blunt the force of the avalanche of false charges of racism, but over time he did it. Now such charges are less common, not because the media has become more honest, but rather because they've figured out the poison doesn't sting the way it used to. Trump's supporters don't care anymore. They can see that Trump is attracting huge numbers of Blacks and Latinos to the GOP, which is hardly the mark of a racist. Others can see it too, and so the secret is out, and fewer Americans than ever before believe the racism charge from the media.

Having launched two tried-and-true smear campaigns against Trump, the Left was, even in Trump's first term, forced to bring out its big guns. I use the term "guns" advisedly, because I am talking here of nothing less than political assassination. Indeed, the Democrats did not wait until the other two smears had failed; they were cooking up the Russia collusion scam even before Trump took office. And let's be clear about what they were going for. They sought to portray Trump's election as illegitimate, his presidency as illegitimate, and Trump himself as a traitor in league with foreign powers.

To put it bluntly, they wanted Trump to be viewed as a traitor and prosecuted for treason, with the understood penalty being life imprisonment or death. Had the scheme worked, this would have indeed been the outcome. This point is critically important to our purpose, because again, we're asking the question of who the real dictator is. As we'll see from this wicked and sordid framing scheme, it's certainly not Trump!

The Russia collusion scheme was audacious in its conception, and breathtaking in the forces mobilized to pull it off. The scheme was concocted inside the Hillary Clinton campaign, almost certainly at Hillary's own direction, but if not at least with her full consent and support. Obama knew about it, and held a meeting in the White House with prominent government officials to work out the execution (again, a word I choose carefully) of the plan. The whole intelligence apparatus of the US government—including FBI director James Comey and CIA director James Clapper—was actively involved.

The media were actively recruited into the scheme, so that journalists willingly printed false and made-up stories, fed to them by the Russia collusion hoaxers, all with a view to nailing Trump. The operating principle behind the media coverage seemed to be that of Joseph Goebbels, who once said that propaganda is not measured according to a standard of truth or falsehood. Propaganda that works—propaganda that is believed—is good propaganda, and everything else is bad propaganda.[53] How telling that even when the Russia collusion hoax was fully exposed—there was no coordination whatever between Trump or even the Trump campaign and the Russians—to my knowledge not a single media outlet retracted its coverage and apologized for the harm caused by its persistent stream of lies.

My friend George Papadopoulos, who was at the time a lowly staffer with the Trump 2016 campaign, was a crucial part of the scheme, and I interviewed him about it for one of my earlier movies, so I'll briefly recount what I learned from him. George was based in London, and he was contacted by a series of shadowy figures—a self-described international businessman named Joseph Mifsud, a Cambridge scholar named Stefan Halper, an Australian diplomat named Alexander Downer. A fourth guy, Charles Tawil, claimed to be an Israeli businessman. All of them, George told me, have ties to Western intelligence agencies, and all met with George with a single mission in mind.

One of them tried to plant in George's mind, with the goal of having him relay the information to the Trump campaign, that the Russians had "dirt" on Hillary Clinton. A couple of them tried to get George to admit that he knew that the Trump campaign was working closely with Russia and Russian intelligence. Another handed George $10,000 in cash, supposedly for a research project, but with the true objective of having George caught with the cash in his luggage upon his return to the US, when the FBI was right there at the airport to grab him and search his luggage, and journalists magically present to record the bust. Fortunately for George, he smelled a rat and therefore left the money behind in Europe with an attorney. So the FBI's staged bust turned out to be a bust.

We learn from George's experience, however, how unscrupulous these people are. They are not above fabricating a crime, and planting the evidence. Quite apart from the various entities I listed above, we can see here that they even got the cooperation of British and Australian intelligence. I'm not suggesting that those agencies had it out for Trump. But quite clearly they were eager to cooperate with their US counterparts, and so they ran errand services for the thugs with badges at the FBI and the CIA.

George is lucky to have survived the scheme—had he sent a single email to the Trump campaign, saying the Russians had dirt on Hillary Clinton, that would have been leaked to every media outlet in the country as prima facie confirmation of Trump being a

Russian asset. And let's always remember that while George was the immediate target, he was not the ultimate target; Trump was. That's the guy that Obama, Hillary, Comey, Clapper, and the whole insidious gang wanted to take out.

It almost worked. Even now I think of the schemers, sulking and seething among themselves and saying, in the words of Guido da Montefeltro, one of the fraudsters deep in Dante's hell, "And oh to think it could have worked."[54] Guido is upset because he tried to defraud God, and it didn't work. The Russia fraudsters and their allies are frustrated because when former FBI director Robert Mueller tried to document the collusion between the Trump campaign and Russia, he found not one scintilla of evidence to support it.

The game was up. Trump survived; he weathered the storm, and with very little support from his own party. The country has moved on from all that. Unfortunately, the dirty gang that carried out the scheme has escaped accountability . . . so far. I believe that if Trump gets a second chance at bat, he should have these schemers investigated with a view to prosecuting them. Trump wasn't the one committing treason—they were. I'm not calling for their execution, although far be it from me to change the ancient wisdom about what should be done with proven traitors.

Given the enormity of the pressure he was under—pressure that began before he assumed office and continued unabated for virtually his entire term—it is amazing that Trump accomplished anything at all. This is even more the case because Trump had such a narrow congressional majority. He had a slim majority in the House and an even slimmer one in the Senate, and these were de jure rather than de facto majorities, because Trump always had a group of Republicans who despised him and sought to undermine him whenever they could, sometimes working in coordination with the Democrats to do it.

Even so, Trump got a significant tax cut passed, and together with the massive maze of regulations that he removed, that launched an economic revival that hummed nicely through the Trump years, until it was stopped in its tracks by the disaster of Covid. Trump also appointed three justices to the Supreme Court, with long-term benefits on many issues, but with one big short-term slam dunk, the termination of abortion-on-demand which had, through the landmark decision of *Roe v. Wade*, been sustained by the Court through Republican and Democratic administrations alike for half a century.

Eventually, thanks to Trump and the Trump majority on the Supreme Court, *Roe* was overturned and became history. That happened in 2022, when Trump had exited the White House and Biden was in the Oval Office. Since the Left and the Democrats are such champions of abortion—in the church of modern progressivism, it has almost become a sacrament—they loathe Trump more for what he has done with this single issue than with any of his other policies. They hate and fear him more now than they did in his first term.

In foreign policy, Trump's record was one of almost unvarnished success. He broke the back of the terrorist group ISIS which had arisen under Obama to supplant Al Qaeda. (With comic exaggeration, Trump liked to quip that Obama was the "founder" of ISIS.) Trump gave the go-ahead for a US military operation in Syria that dispatched Islamic State terror chief Abu Bakr al-Baghdadi, noting, as a matter of helpful detail, that al-Baghdadi "died like a dog."[55]

Trump also torpedoed Obama's Iran Deal—a sycophantic giveaway to one of America's most dangerous adversaries—and approved a successful drone strike that killed Iran's top military commander, General Qasem Soleimani. Most important, Trump dealt with world dictators like Putin, Xi, and Kim Jong Un in a manner that ensured that bad things did not happen. Putin respected Trump and was, at least in Trump's account to me and my family, somewhat intimidated by Trump. Putin waited for Biden before he made the decision to invade Ukraine.

The most striking thing about Trump's achievements, in the economic, cultural and foreign policy spheres, is how effortless they seemed. Trump displayed an almost zany ability to shift the goalposts of the possible. He succeeded without apparently trying too hard, and in the process embarrassed those who have studied and prepared and then tried all their lives without a single success.

The pompous effete establishment watched Trump perform his presidential circus act in virtual disbelief. They were like the Pharisees witnessing Jesus perform miracles, and far from being impressed and going over to his side, their envy and hatred of him grew all the more, and they resolved with even greater determination to finish this man off once and for all. It wasn't because he was a dictator. It's because he was ruining the show for all of them, and if they let him go on he might just put the whole lot of them out of business.

CHAPTER 4

A NEW FORM OF TYRANNY

If you want a picture of the future, imagine a boot stamping on a human face—forever.[56]

—George Orwell, *1984*

The United States is facing, for the first time in its history, the problem of tyranny. Of course America was, to a degree, under a form of tyranny when it was a British colony. Americans were under the control of the king and the British parliament, and even if the degree of control was never very extreme, in principle Americans were obliged to conform to foreign direction in all matters. This was the provocation for the American Revolution, a revolution to establish self-government and individual freedom.

But now America is, once again, confronting the danger of moving toward a tyrannical society—of becoming a police state. Both sides agree on this! The Left and the Democrats accuse Trump of leading the tyrannical movement, but as we have seen, Trump is no dictator. Trump is not Caesar, and nothing he has done or even said suggests he wants to be. But if Trump isn't Caesar, who is? If Trump isn't the tyranny, where is the threat of tyranny coming from?

In this chapter, I'll show that it comes from the Left and from the Democrats. They represent Caesar, albeit a new kind of Caesar. What makes the new Caesar so dangerous is that he disguises himself—he pretends not to be a Caesar. What I mean is that the new police state that is being imposed on us marches behind the banner of democracy and rule of law. It poses as the defender and savior of democracy, and it portrays Trump and those of us who are trying to take it down as "enemies of democracy."

Admittedly, Caesar himself camouflaged his imperial ambitions. In Mark Antony's speech following Caesar's assassination, Antony says:

> You all did see that on the Lupercal,
> I thrice presented him with a kingly crown,
> Which he did thrice refuse. Was this ambition?[57]

The rhetorical question has the presumed answer, "No." The crowd is supposed to arrive at this conclusion from the observation that Caesar made a triple disavowal of the offer to become a monarch. The crowd is struck dumb because the ambition to be an emperor is expected in a man of Caesar's stature. Who in his position wouldn't want to rule the roost? Why would he refuse power in this way?

But Antony himself knows why Caesar disavowed the crown, and so does the skeptical aristocrat Casca, who is also in the audience. These men recognize that Caesar's refusal was not a suspension of ambition but an exercise of it. Caesar knew that ever since the Romans drove out the Tarquin kings, tyranny was detested by the people. For Caesar to show deference to this public sentiment was a political necessity. Caesar recognized the best way to be an emperor was to exercise the powers of kingship without the title. In sum, Caesar was a very good actor, Antony was his public relations man, and the crowd fell for it. The correct answer to Antony's question is, "Yes."

So, too, the architects of the American police state conceal their true motives and proclaim themselves to be champions of freedom and constitutional democracy. But how do we know that they are subverting it? Let's begin by looking at what the most far-seeing prophets and chroniclers of modern tyranny have to say about the defining characteristics of police states. I am thinking specifically here of George Orwell, author of *Animal Farm* and *1984*, the Czech dissident Vaclav Havel, author of *The Power of the Powerless*, and Alexander Solzhenitsyn, author of *The Gulag Archipelago*, the authoritative history of the Soviet police state.

Solzhenitsyn tells us we should not think gulags are only possible in the Soviet Union or in some remote faraway place. They are possible, he insists, "everywhere on earth."[58] And the reason is that tyranny is a human problem. Always and everywhere, they are people who seek to rule tyrannically over others. What makes modern tyranny worse, however, is that it is comprehensive tyranny.

The old czars (inheriting their name from Caesar) merely sought to control the apparatus of government, but they didn't care what you ate or where you went or how you made your living or how you worshipped or even what you said in public—as long as you didn't threaten their rule. Modern tyranny, however, aims to run your life and ultimately control it in all respects. That's because modern tyranny is ideological tyranny—tyranny in service of an ideological scheme.

The tyrants Solzhenitsyn writes about are socialists and Communists; theirs is the tyranny of the political Left. The reason that modern tyrannies, from Communism to Nazism, come from the Left is that the Left has formulated an ideological blueprint for society that involves giving the state increasing—and in the end ultimate—power. To quote Mussolini's definition of fascism,

"Everything in the state, nothing outside the state, nothing above the state."[59] Today, this is the philosophy of the Left—not only in America, but worldwide.

Most people do not see the arrival of tyranny in their society because at first it happens not to them but to other people. And so they tell themselves, "It can't happen here" or "It can't happen to me." And when it does happen to them, when the police come knocking at their door to make an arrest, they protest, "There must be some mistake" or "You have the wrong person." They are sure they will soon clear up the matter, not realizing that there is nothing to clear up, and that they are being removed from society because they are perceived as enemies of the state. The regime wants them gone.

For some Americans, all of this might seem surreal, because surely in America people don't get locked up without due process and some legal basis for their criminal convictions. But Solzhenitsyn points out that the legal process in any society is infinitely elastic. There are always ways to control the legal process by controlling who is the judge and who is on the panel issuing the final sentence and even which laws are invoked in what way to justify the sentence. Ordinary people see a paneled room, a judge in robes, and they hear the mumbo-jumbo of legal discourse, and they assume that a legitimate legal process is under way.

Solzhenitsyn mentions a Soviet jurist named Andrei Vyshinsky who, "availing himself of the most flexible dialectics," made the case that "it is never possible for mortal men to establish absolute truth, but relative truth only." And therefore, when people are locked up or shot, no one can be absolutely sure if they are guilty or innocent. It is useless to seek absolute evidence, for evidence is always relative. The only question for the regime is: How much evidence is enough? Millions of political prisoners were locked up—and many executed—under the Vyshinsky doctrine.[60]

Of the modern tyrannical regime, Havel writes in *The Power of the Powerless*, "It touches people at every step, but it does so with ideological gloves on. This is why life in the system is so thoroughly permeated with hypocrisy and lies. The arbitrary abuse of power is called observing the legal code. The lack of free expression becomes the highest form of freedom. Farcical elections become the highest form of democracy. Banning independent thought becomes the most scientific of worldviews. It falsifies the past. It falsifies the present. And it falsifies the future. Because the regime is captive to its own lies, it must falsify everything."[61]

Orwell makes the point that modern tyranny requires a gang or a political party to carry it out, in part because one man, however strong, can only dominate a handful of other men, and perhaps a lot of women and children. How do you control and regulate the lives of millions? You need a massive operation to do it. And Orwell suggests that typically there is an "inner party" made up of spies and police and government officials, and then an "outer party" made up of intellectuals and journalists who do the regime's bidding, such as justifying its show trials and propagandizing its fictitious accomplishments.[62]

"Intellectuals," Orwell writes, "are more totalitarian in outlook than the common people. Most of them are perfectly ready for dictatorial methods, secret police, systematic falsification of history, etc. so long as they feel it is on 'our' side." Tyranny comes in stages, Orwell says, little by little, and then more and more, until the regime he calls Big Brother is finally in place, symbolized by the grim image of "a boot stamping on a human face—forever."[63] This prospect we might perhaps call not just a police state but a police planet. Global tyranny!

We're all familiar with tyranny in China, North Korea, Venezuela, and the old Soviet Union. But here? Yes, here. And how do we know this? Let's consider the defining features of the classic police state, and ask which of those features do we now see in America.

First, mass surveillance of citizens. Check!

Second, an elaborate regime of censorship of political views that run athwart, or are inconvenient to, the regime. Check!

Third, ideological indoctrination in schools and in the media. Check!

Fourth, criminalization of political differences and the existence of political prisoners who are locked up for their dissident views. Check!

Finally, the prosecution, incarceration, and attempted assassination of leading political opponents, so as to consolidate the power of the regime. Check!

My point is not that the police state is coming; it is that it is already here. Of course, it is possible to quibble with the checklist given above—censorship, for instance, is coming from digital platforms and not directly from the government, the January 6 defendants aren't really political prisoners, and so on—but even so, it's hard to deny that at least some of the defining features of tyranny have become familiar and even accepted features of American life. When I first came to America, I had no problem calling us the "free world," and then on the other side there was the "unfree world," but now those distinctions are blurred. We're not a full-fledged police state, but we're headed alarmingly in that direction.

I'm sorry to say that, in this chapter, I won't be able to give a full account of the emerging police state. I made a movie on this subject last year. It's called—you guessed it—*Police State*, and I invite you to check it out for the full story. But I will here identify the ideological origin of the police state, show how it really got going under Obama, and how it escalated dramatically under the Biden regime, with the full embrace of the political Left and the leadership of the Democratic Party.

Coming in as an outsider, Trump may have underestimated the depth and dishonesty of this tyrannical system, which fully showed its hand only after he left office. Even so, Trump has resisted its machinations at every turn, not only when it set its sights on him, and his great achievement is to reveal the corruption and rottenness of our leading institutions—notably the police agencies of the government, but also health institutions and even the US military—and expose them as part of the machinery of the police state. Without Trump, virtually all of it would still be hidden. The Left and the Democrats would have consolidated their tyrannical power to such an extent that, when the police state finally went public, it would be too late for anyone to stop it.

Think about Soviet tyranny under Stalin. When they came to arrest you at the train station, they didn't have to give you a reason. Your name was on a list, and that was it; you're finished. Only a police state in the process of establishing itself needs to maintain a façade, because it wants to avoid early detection at a stage when it can be rebuffed and shut down. We're now at a stage when we still can prevail over the emerging tyranny, but time is running out, and it's going to take a man like Trump to lead a successful turnaround.

The roots of the American police state go back a full century to the early progressive movement, so they long precede Trump. The progressives had this in common with the Communists and the socialists: they rejected the principles of the American founding, and they believed in the all-powerful centralized state, what they called the "administrative state." They envisioned such a state being run by trusted experts, people like, well, themselves.

Here's progressive icon E. A. Ross, from his book aptly titled *Social Control*, "The state is an organization that puts the wise minority in the saddle." Herbert Croly, Edward Alsworth Ross, John Dewey, and their political candidate Woodrow Wilson, all believed it. And while in theory the state is supposed to be democratically run by the people, Ross candidly admits that "as a matter of fact the state, when it becomes paternal and develops on the administrative side, is able in a measure to guide the society it professes to obey." It becomes, in a sense, "an independent center of social power."[64]

Ross's book was published in 1918. So the theoretical foundations for the progressive police state were laid around the same time that they were laid for Soviet Bolshevism and for the fascist and Nazi parties in Europe. But it took a long time for recognizable police state techniques to begin in America, where there is plenty of constitutional ballast—a written Constitution with an enumerated Bill of Rights, separation of powers, and checks and balances—to slow the process down. The progressives had to figure out a way to overcome that, and it took successive progressive administrations—Woodrow Wilson, FDR, LBJ—to slowly accomplish that.

Obama was the pioneer of the American police state. He got it going, even if only to the nascent or infant stage. Obama has acknowledged despotic tendencies. As reported in the *New York Times*, he once said it would be so much easier to be the president of China.[65] Ah, yes. That's because the president of China is a dictator. He doesn't have to answer to Congress, and he is largely unaccountable to publish opinion. He just does what he wants, and I'm sure he has lots of "wingmen" and little czars to help him execute his grand designs.

Recall that Obama used his IRS to go after conservative and Tea Party groups, and that my own campaign finance prosecution was under Obama. The key to my case was not that I exceeded the campaign finance limit. I did, but it was out of zeal to help a college friend. It was a first-time offense and there was no quid pro quo.

No American has ever been charged, let alone locked up, for doing what I did.

Justice isn't simply a question of whether one breaks the law. It also involves proportionality—the penalty should fit the crime—and also equality of treatment: one should receive roughly the same punishment as anyone else who did the same thing. But Obama did not hesitate to deploy against me the classic police state technique of selective prosecution, which has now become commonplace under the Biden regime. My real "crime" was making a film that made Obama look really bad.

Let's review the key developments of the Democratic police state, excluding the legal cases against Trump, which will be covered in the next chapter. The first impeachment had a dual purpose. One purpose was to cover up the massive stream of money the Biden family has taken in from foreign entities, from China to Russia to Ukraine. This is what Trump had asked Zelenskyy over the phone to investigate. Joe Biden had not only gotten a local prosecutor fired who was looking into corruption at the Burisma energy company—which had put Hunter Biden on its board and was paying him $83,000 a month—but he had also boasted about it. Trump did nothing more than say: Why not look into it?

Let's note that, when this happened, the FBI was already in possession of Hunter Biden's laptop, which chronicled in excruciating detail the crimes and corruption of Joe Biden's family. I say Joe Biden's family because Joe was the head of this domestic mafia. It was his influence that was being peddled; he, after all, was point man for Ukraine when he was vice president. Hunter Biden was merely the bag man collecting the money that would then, by Hunter's own admission, be shared with Joe. Ten percent for the Big Guy!

Even so, the congressional Democrats made it look like Trump was the one trying to get his political opponent prosecuted. Trump was engaged in election interference! Thus, with the first impeachment the Democrats hoped to kill two birds with one stone: kill off the inquiry into Joe Biden's corruption, and kill off Trump's chances of running for re-election. This was the real election interference. But unfortunately for the perpetrators, it failed. The Senate refused to convict Trump. It was a bruising process, but he survived.

For years afterward, Biden would go around falsely claiming that Trump threatened to withhold aid from Ukraine if it didn't have its prosecutor investigate him. The fact, of course, is that Biden threatened to withhold a billion dollars in US aid if Ukraine didn't fire the prosecutor investigating his son's company. This is what Havel meant when he said that the modern police state falsifies everything.

Next up, Covid, which Jane Fonda tellingly described as "God's gift to the Left."[66] I think this is also true in two quite separate senses. Forget the silly parlor-room debate over whether Trump was right to call it the "China virus." Of course he was; the virus came from China. From the Spanish flu to the Ebola Virus to the West Nile virus, it is customary to name viruses based on the places from which they originated. Move on!

The important point is that Covid crushed the Trump economy, and thus undermined Trump's own chances for re-election. Admittedly, this was because Trump acquiesced in the decision of many—not all but most—states to lock down their economies. Until then, Trump had a roaring economy that would surely aid in, if not guarantee, his re-election. Trump had every interest in opposing the shutdowns, which he could have done. But he did not.

Why not? There is only one answer to this question. Trump trusted the health authorities who told him this was a global pandemic which had the potential to cost millions of American lives. The experts—most prominently Dr. Anthony Fauci—told Trump to "trust the science" and "trust me." And Trump did. In fact, he had no reason not to. Fauci had been in his job since the Reagan era. Who knew that the health authorities had also been infected with political, financial, and ideological corruption?

We know this in retrospect, but we didn't know it at the time. And so Trump did the right thing and temporarily approved a shutdown. Politically, it cost him dearly, as he knew it would. And here is proof that Trump is not the selfish guy his critics and adversaries make him out to be. He's not merely out for himself. He knowingly jeopardized his own chances for re-election for the sole purpose of overcoming the pandemic and saving American lives. This is not—I repeat not—the conduct of a dictator or tyrant, who is normally indifferent to the public welfare, especially when it undermines his own.

Covid, it seems, originated from the Wuhan Lab in Wuhan, China. There is continuing debate about this, but the evidence now favors the lab leak theory. And this is incriminating for Fauci and the US health authorities because they had been using taxpayer money to fund so-called "gain of function" research. This gain of function research is aimed at studying viruses by making them more lethal and contagious. Some of this research is outlawed in the United States, but the US labs were outsourcing it to the Wuhan Lab and working in collaboration with the Chinese scientists there. The risks, of course, were not merely that dangerous viruses might get out and kill millions of people, but also that the research was under the supervision of the Chinese government and the Chinese Communist Party, aiding their efforts in making biological weapons.

In a classic police state maneuver, Fauci sought to conceal the likelihood of a lab leak. He directed some leading virologists to write a paper downplaying and dismissing that prospect, and asserting instead that Covid most likely had a natural origin—it came from a so-called wet market in Wuhan. The virologists were on the US government payroll to the tune of millions of dollars, so not surprisingly they obliged. And then Fauci, who had commissioned the paper, read it beforehand, even edited it, held a press conference at which he held it up, pretending that he had just read it in the scientific literature, and used it to "debunk" the lab leak theory.[67] Fauci's deception was willingly promulgated by the media. Some of these were useful idiots, of course, who thought they were merely "following the science."

Depressing though it is to have such subterfuge going on at the high levels of the US government—and through the health authorities, which people implicitly trust with their safety and their lives—I suppose it is also encouraging at some level. As I suggested earlier, a full-blown police state doesn't need to engage in such stagecraft. It doesn't need fake papers and fake press conferences. The Ministry of Propaganda simply puts out a statement, "Covid came from a wet market in Wuhan," and anyone who says otherwise is promptly carted away and jailed. We're not there yet, which is a good thing.

Fauci also trumpeted the "six feet rule" for social distancing. He didn't come up with it, but he recommended it, and as the chief health official in the country, his recommendation carried tremendous weight. Pretty soon it became the basis for a whole regimen of social controls based upon this supposedly scientific criterion for reducing the spread of deadly viruses. Recently, though, Fauci admitted that there was no scientific basis for the six feet rule. "It sort of just appeared," he said, "that six feet is going to be the distance."[68] Basically, someone made it up! This is evidently what "follow the science" really amounted to.

But why? What is the rationale for making stuff up? Who benefits from it, or in the Latin phrase, cui bono? Here again, there is a compelling answer. The political establishment, mainly made up of Democrats but also consisting of some anti-Trump and Never

Trump Republicans, wanted to come up with a way to change the rules of the 2020 election in a manner that would prevent the re-election of Trump. And the six feet rule provided a perfect rationale. After all, if people cannot stand closer than six feet to one another, how can you have in-person voting when people customarily stand in line and wait their turn to vote?

The six feet rule, in other words, was the fabricated basis for absentee ballots and mail-in ballot dropboxes. And the whole Covid rigmarole—from the six feet rule to the origin of the virus to the mask and vaccine mandates—became the arena for massive social media censorship, originated and encouraged by the health authorities and the mainstream media.

The censorship was ostensibly to curtail "misinformation" and "disinformation," but, as it turned out, the health authorities themselves were the primary source of misinformation and disinformation. Rochelle Walensky, director of the Center for Disease Control, famously said if you take the vaccine, you can't get Covid and you can't give anyone Covid.[69] False. The six feet rule is "following the science." False. We know Covid had a natural origin. False again. The censorship, in other words, existed for the purpose of protecting these false narratives.

To see the sprawling tentacles of tyranny—the full vast group of malefactors that are involved with the police state—consider how the censorship regime operates. Digital platforms create portals. Government agencies, from the State Department to the Department of Homeland Security to the health authorities, all feed tens of thousands, if not millions, of names into the portals. These are the supposed purveyors of misinformation that need to be suppressed or banned. But to conceal its dirty hands, the government typically doesn't deal with the platforms directly. It feeds its names to nonprofit groups such as the Virality Project or the

Stanford Internet Observatory. Those groups then do the handoff to the digital platforms.

And the media cheers the whole enterprise! Consider this February 18, 2021 article by Charlie Warzel in the *New York Times*. Titled, "Don't Go Down the Rabbit Hole," the Op-ed is subtitled, "Critical thinking, as we're taught to do it, isn't helping in the fight again misinformation." We're told that asking questions, doing your own research, making up your own mind are all "fundamentally flawed."[70] The basic message of the article is to do what the government tells you! So if you're wondering how people became police state apparatchiks in Stalin's Russia or Hitler's Germany, this is how. Charlie Warzel would have fit right in as a regular writer for *Pravda* or with Goebbels's Ministry of Propaganda.

If Covid helped Democrats unlevel the playing field for the 2020 election—all to prevent Trump from winning again—so did the censorship of the Hunter Biden laptop story. Of course the media knew the laptop was real. If they had any doubts, they could have clarified with the FBI, which was in possession of the laptop for over a year and also knew the laptop was real. Later, of course, the FBI would itself introduce the laptop in Hunter Biden's gun trial, and confirm that it had been authenticated by the agency from the very beginning.

The fifty-one top intelligence officials—some of the highest past and present figures in the intelligence community, some of them Republicans—also knew the laptop was real, even though they all signed a letter publicly claiming it had the "hallmarks" of a Russian disinformation operation. In truth, they were engaged in some disinformation of their own, to help Joe Biden get across the finish line. And to this day, not one of these corrupt and indeed treasonous officials has so much as apologized or retracted their knowingly false statement, which might have tipped the balance in a close national election.

This brings me to the last main exhibit of this chapter, which is January 6. The people who went into the Capitol on January 6, 2021 obviously felt the 2020 election was stolen. They had good reasons to suspect it was, and a year and a half later, when I released *2000 Mules*, they and many others could see for themselves that these instincts were right. But I deal with election fraud in a later chapter.

Here, I simply ask the question. Here was a routine political demonstration, not substantially different from leftists who have many times invaded congressional offices, taken over courthouses and occupied official government buildings more times than anyone can count. In fact, this had been going on, at a scale that dwarfed January 6, for months in the wake of the death of George Floyd.

So how could a protest that was tame compared with all of that—one in which no one brought any weapons and no one was killed except Trump supporter Ashli Babbitt, shot in cold blood by a Capitol Police officer—now suddenly be characterized as an "insurrection," an attempt to overthrow the US government, the most serious assault on the nation's Capitol since the Civil War, and an unprecedented attempt, provoked by a sitting President, to subvert democracy?

Trump never urged anyone to go inside the Capitol. Yet, since then Trump has been criminally indicted by Special Counsel Jack Smith for supposedly trying to overturn election results and subvert our constitutional system, and thousands of January 6 protesters, most of them nonviolent, have been subjected to ruthless prosecution, lengthy pre-trial detainments, and ultimately long prison sentences on the basis that they somehow "attacked democracy." If all this seems surreal, a theater of the absurd, we must still ask, how is it even possible?

To answer this question, we need to review how the intelligence agencies of the police state set up the Gretchen Whitmer kidnapping "plot." The plot, it should be noted, was revealed right before the 2020 election, another scam aimed at conveying the false message to the American people that "right wing extremism" of the MAGA kind was a demonstrable threat to democracy.

In reality, the FBI cooked up the plot. FBI agents found a bunch of angry rednecks who were sick of Covid lockdowns and were talking smack about Michigan Governor Gretchen Whitmer. These guys were big-talking losers. They were not about to do anything, on their own, to Whitmer. They were utterly incapable of carrying out any kind of plot.

But that's where the FBI came in, to organize the scheme, to supply the materials, to infiltrate the gang of perpetrators, to drive them on reconnaissance trips, to provide the ammunition and the opportunity. There were just as many FBI agents and informants involved as perpetrators. Moreover, Whitmer herself was in on the scheme. She was never in any danger. She approved and helped coordinate the "recons" planned and staged by the feds in conjunction with Michigan State Police and the Attorney General's office.

Later, of course, Whitmer went on TV and put on a big act, pretending that she had been in grave danger and that the amazing FBI had busted a genuine threat to her life. The media played along, whooping up the narrative that MAGA extremism posed the greatest threat to the safety of American citizens—an even greater threat than ISIS. The whole Whitmer scheme was an orchestrated hoax to produce a political outcome, and the poor men were sacrificial lambs.[71] Fortunately, most of them were acquitted in jury trials because the jury understood precisely what went on.

Then the FBI division chief who oversaw the Whitmer kidnapping hoax, Steven D'Antuono, was transferred to Washington, DC to oversee the January 6 operation. What we know for sure is that the crowd entering the Capitol was infiltrated with undercover agents from a whole range of government agencies, from the FBI to Homeland Security to the DC police. The government refuses to reveal to what extent its own people participated in the Capitol incursion: who took down the barriers, who egged the crowd to make its way in.

We do know, because we see it on video, that once inside, the protesters were greeting and shaking hands with police, in some cases even being escorted by them. At no point do we ever see anyone in authority demanding that the protesters evacuate the building. Finally, we know for a fact that the January 6 Committee suppressed any information that contradicted its premise that Trump and his followers were entirely to blame, and that they were attempting a takedown of the US government itself.

Again, cui bono? While there is no question that an official proceeding was under way, and that it was paused because of the big ruckus at the Capitol, hardly anyone pauses to consider: what precisely was that proceeding? The conventional answer—the January 6 Committee's approved answer—is that it was the certification of Joe Biden and Kamala Harris.

But this is not the proceeding that was under way and that was in fact stopped. Rather, the proceeding that ground to a halt, and was never resumed, was the challenging of the authenticity of the ballot totals in the swing or battleground states. Republicans were questioning Georgia, Arizona, Michigan, Wisconsin, Pennsylvania. And by common acknowledgement on the part of the Republicans who were doing that, they lost the will to continue after the events of January 6. It was now deemed an "insurrection," and further inquiries were now considered a incitement to further violence and a danger to the democratic process itself.

So Pelosi and Schumer got what they wanted—a sudden end to the congressional inquiries about election fraud. The January 6 Committee—bipartisan in name but uniformly made up of members who despised Trump—got its way, which was not merely the ejection of Trump from the White House but an opportunity to now blame him and perhaps even provide the basis for charging him criminally. Finally the rhetoric of "insurrection," overstated and absurd as it was—how does one even carry out an insurrection without a single weapon?—served the very useful purpose of justifying a new and even more comprehensive regime of censorship.

Not only did Congress stop questioning the 2020 election; after January 6, no one was permitted to do so, on pain of being permanently banned at Facebook, Instagram, YouTube, and Twitter. Trump himself was thrown off Facebook, Instagram, and Twitter and his content was routinely censored on YouTube. Moreover, these digital platforms expanded their portfolio of censored topics beyond even Covid and election fraud. Going forward, they censored disfavored views about abortion, about lesbian, gay, and trans issues, and climate change. Political debate in general became unfree, and largely remained so until Elon Musk blew a huge hole in the censorship apparatus by purchasing and rebranding Twitter.

January 6 not only inaugurated a second impeachment and subsequent prosecution of Trump; it not only resulted in the extravagant prosecutions of thousands of Trump supporters; but it also opened up a new era of surveillance and prosecution of conservatives, Republicans, patriots, and Christians.

Now the FBI and the intelligence agencies felt emboldened to charge pro-lifers who were doing nothing more than standing and praying at abortion clinics of obstructing services and thus violating the so-called Face Act. Some pro-life men and women are currently facing, or serving, years in prison for that. As an example, my friend Bevelyn Beatty, who was featured in *Police State*, got forty-one months for doing nothing more than shouting slogans outside the Planned Parenthood clinic in New York. The FBI also began monitoring moms at school board meetings, supposedly because their challenges to school boards and teachers for allowing pornography and LGBTQ propaganda into schools posed a threat to the safety of school officials.

The expansion of surveillance, censorship and political prosecutions—all defining hallmarks of a police state—shows how January 6 became, for the Left and the Democrats, a Reichstag Fire opportunity. When a foreign communist burned the German parliament or Reichstag in 1933, Hitler and the Nazis used the provocation, which some say was orchestrated by the Nazis themselves, to justify an elaborate regime of suppression of civil liberties.[72] And that's precisely how the Democrats used January 6.

As a postscript to these events, it's worth mentioning that in the days following January 6, the top military officer of the United States, General Mark Milley, took it upon himself to call his Chinese counterpart and assure him that the United States was not going to attack China, and that even if Trump gave the order, he, General Milley, would give the Chinese a heads-up in advance. Moreover, according to Bob Woodward of the *Washington Post*, Milley also asked senior defense officials to swear an oath that Milley had to be consulted if Trump gave an order to launch nuclear weapons.[73]

While Milley would later downplay the significance of what he did, pretending that it was a normal exercise of his responsibilities, it's quite clear that he was acting in coordination with Democrats in Congress who had proclaimed Trump "unhinged" and not to be trusted even with his duties as commander in chief. Milley in effect became the shadow president, at least in terms of usurping Trump's authority in this crucial area.

And so we see, once again, that Trump was not the dictator—all dictators make sure they have complete command of the military—and, on the contrary, the military leadership was already answering to the regime that was in the process of taking over from Trump. Milley understood very well what he had to do to keep his job, which he did under the incoming Biden regime.

The Democratic police state under the Biden regime has now become fairly well entrenched. Trump might have exposed their fangs, but their fangs are ugly and powerful even in the face of greater public awareness. The Democrats are in the position of Macbeth, who says:

> I am in blood, Stepped in so far that I should wade no more
> Returning were as tedious as go o'er.[74]

What Macbeth means is that he is too far gone down the road of crimes and mayhem. Even if he's tempted to return and go back, it's too difficult. It's easier to just keep going, to heap new crimes on top of the old ones. The Democrats, like Macbeth, will not quit of their own accord. Tyrannical schemes brought them to power in 2020 and they are relying on the tyrannical playbook to keep them there. Only one Republican—Trump—has pledged to stop them, and only he has the strength and the will to do it.

CHAPTER 5

LEGAL ASSASSINATION

_____

Sic semper tyrannis.

—John Wilkes Booth

This chapter is about three types of assassination. The first, which we have already encountered in connection with Trump, is political assassination, which also involves character assassination. The second is legal assassination, sometimes called "lawfare." The term is appropriate, because it is derived from warfare. This is an attempt to use lawlessness, under the guise of law, to bankrupt, ruin, defame, and even imprison a dangerous political opponent. In extreme cases this opponent might even face life imprisonment, which is a legal equivalent of the death penalty. (Murderers are often given the death penalty or life in prison, which some people say is a fate worse than death.) And finally, when all else fails, there is actual assassination.

These three types of assassination are connected, and typically one leads to another. During the English Civil War, King Charles I, who admittedly was a tyrant, was subjected to a lengthy volley of complaints and accusations. This was character assassination aimed at producing his overthrow—political assassination. Then he was tried by the Rump Parliament, but it was a bogus trial, mainly consisting of crimes that were made up solely in order to convict him. Charles was only guilty of laws passed ex post facto by the Parliament; he was then retroactively found to have violated those laws. Finally, Charles was executed, a supposedly lawful penalty for his crimes, but since the crimes themselves were bogus the execution amounted to an assassination. The point is that while Charles was indeed a tyrant, the process of his deposition and murder were no less lawless—no less tyrannical—than Charles himself.

More recently, and closer to home, John Wilkes Booth assassinated President Abraham Lincoln at Ford's Theater on April 14, 1865. The Southern Democrats who led the Confederacy had been blackening Lincoln's character for years, calling him a "gorilla" and a "tyrant." Secession itself amounted to a kind of lawfare. It had no legal or constitutional basis—Lincoln's only "crime" was that he had won the 1860 election, and secession was nothing more than a spurious attempt to invalidate the result of that election. And of course secession led rapidly to war: lawfare became warfare!

Finally, Booth murdered Lincoln, as part of a plot to kill the President, the Vice President, and the Secretary of State. Booth and his co-conspirators were Confederates. Their minds had been poisoned by years of propaganda. Booth genuinely believed Lincoln was a tyrant. His political motive was to get rid of Lincoln and energize the Confederacy to fight on even after the surrender at Appomattox. After shooting Lincoln, Booth jumped to the stage of the theater and shouted, "Sic semper tyrannis," which means "So it goes with tyrants." This was hardly a phrase that Booth picked up in acting school—it was the motto of the state of Virginia, the leading state of the Confederacy.

With Trump, character assassination came first. When it proved insufficient, it metamorphosed into lawfare. We see this with the Stormy Daniels matter, which began as a sex scandal, aimed at showing Trump to be a philanderer and low-life. Later, Manhattan

District Attorney Alvin Bragg used the same set of facts—Trump's lawyer paid Stormy Daniels to sign a Non-Disclosure Agreement or NDA—to concoct a two-tiered crime: alteration of business records (a misdemeanor) and an attempt to violate federal campaign finance laws (a felony). We might reasonably ask how Bragg gets so much out of so little. But he got a jury conviction out of it, and for this entirely legal and legitimate transaction—NDAs are perfectly legal and wealthy individuals and businesses do them all the time— Trump faces thirty-four felony convictions and potentially many years in prison. For a man of his age, this would be tantamount to a life sentence, a legal assassination. But even that was not enough, because just a few weeks ago Trump was the target of an assassin's bullet that should have taken his life but almost miraculously only grazed his ear.

One might say that the wicked and lawless regime that has been out to get Trump from the outset is taking no chances. This regime—run by Obama, Pelosi, Schumer, Biden, Harris, the whole Democratic gang—represents precisely the lawlessness that Lincoln warned about in his Lyceum speech. The only difference is that the regime now controls the levers of law. So it deploys law itself to abuse the process of law. It is a legal abomination. And when even this fails, it does what the Confederacy did with Booth: it poisons the minds of unstable and disturbed individuals so that one of them, in this case a twenty-year-old man named Thomas Crooks, takes the law into his own hands and attempts to kill a former and potentially future President.

Think of the unrelenting demonization of Trump that began in 2015, and has now gone on for almost a decade. Remember the Shakespeare in the Park play, adapted from *Julius Caesar*, in which Trump (portrayed as the modern-day embodiment of Caesar) was stabbed to death on stage? Remember comedian Kathy Griffin sharing a meme in which she holds up Trump's bloody, severed head? The comparisons between Trump and Hitler coming from Hillary Clinton and leading Democrats are simply too numerous to count. Just a couple of weeks before the attempted assassination, Joe Biden posted on X, "Donald Trump is a genuine threat to this nation. He's a threat to our freedom. He's a threat to our democracy. He's literally a threat to everything America stands for." And around the same time, Nancy Pelosi said on MSNBC that 2024 is "not a normal election," and that Trump "must be stopped."[75] Surely Crooks was heavily exposed to this diet of murderous anti-Trump propaganda.

And most likely, he believed it. Whatever Crooks's ideology, his motive quite obviously was to get rid of a man he believed to be a danger to democracy and to the country. Quite likely he saw himself as the intrepid soldier who had the foresight to take Hitler out before he could unleash a world war and murder millions of Jews as part of his "final solution." In other words, Crooks believed the lie that Trump is like Hitler, like Caesar, like Napoleon. Crooks, too, sought to make the point that Booth did—sic semper tyrannis.

In a way, Crooks was more sincere than the Democrats whose evil slander he absorbed. Immediately following the failed assassination attempt, leading Democrats all offered "thoughts and prayers" to Trump. They said they were hoping for his quick recovery. But wait a minute! If Trump was truly Hitler—if they genuinely believed Trump was akin to Hitler—then they should be celebrating the assassination attempt, as indeed some on the Left did. Their only regret should have been that Crooks missed. Thus there is an unavoidable conflict between their premise (Trump is Hitler) and their conclusion (We are praying for Hitler to recover quickly). Either the premise is false or the conclusion is false. My view is that the Democrats never truly believed Trump is Hitler—in fact, they know he isn't—but they use that base slander to demonize and dispatch a dangerous political opponent. The danger Trump poses is not to liberty or to the republic but only to them and to their tyrannical schemes.

What I intend to show in this chapter is not merely the diabolical schemes to destroy Trump by locking him up for life, or outright killing him, but also how Trump has largely foiled these schemes. It seemed impossible for a man facing ninety-one criminal charges and hundreds of years in prison to have the whole legal barrage deflected, turned back or tossed out, what podcaster Megyn Kelly calls the "inside straight." Who else could not only plough through the barrage undeterred, but even (at least to date) prevail? Any other Republican—any other politician—facing ten charges would exit the race, implode psychologically, and become a political nonentity and liability, never mentioned by his own side again.

Trump, however, has shown he has the mettle to fight and to win. In a way, Trump found a way to turn even his vices into political virtues. Consider, for instance, Trump's ego. Trump said in his early career that all successful people have a big ego. He doesn't regard his ego as a liability but, in a business sense, as a motivating asset. But now, in the political minefield, his ego serves a greater— one might even say nobler—purpose. In a weird way, Trump's ego has been a form of psychological self-protection through the political and legal trauma of the past several years. Trump's ego is his own personal wall, insulating him from the pressures that would surely debilitate, if not destroy, a normal person. We should be grateful for his conceit; it helps him stay on track and forge resolutely ahead.

Drawing on inner strength and creativity, Trump used the lawfare against him to put the legal system itself on trial, and he exposed the sham machinations of a whole procession of Democratic prosecutors, judges, and juries, all acting at the direction and behest of the

Biden-Harris regime. In a way, he vindicated his character through these cases, because he showed the American public that this is all they have on him, and if this is the best they can do, Trump must in fact be one of the cleanest, least corrupt figures on the whole landscape. Who else could withstand such extensive scrutiny and come out almost entirely unscathed? Only Trump! This man has lived his entire adult life in the public eye and, as it turns out, he has had very little to hide.

And as we'll see, even the assassination attempt proved to be to the benefit of Trump. First, it showed that he was a person important enough to be targeted. Assassination, after all, is the sincerest form of flattery. Consider Biden or Harris, or even Romney or Paul Ryan. Who would want to assassinate them? It would be a waste of effort, and of ammunition. There is a reason no one ever attempted to assassinate Jimmy Carter. Trump joined a rare and illustrious list of presidents or would-be presidents who faced assassination: Lincoln, Teddy Roosevelt, JFK, RFK, Reagan. And even in this elite company, Trump showed his mettle by the instinctive way he responded to the assassin's bullets. Here, in a single moment, Trump showed his true greatness and proved he has more genuine virtue and character than all his critics combined.

People who do wicked deeds to get rid of their opponents often try to avoid having to go down the base and murderous trail. They, too, have a conscience, and they would prefer to take some other, less vicious path, if they could. It is in this spirit that I understand a series of articles, published over the past few years, calling for Trump to go into exile. Here's *Politico* in 2020: "The Case for Political Exile for Donald Trump." The article begins, "What is to be done with Donald Trump?" Answer: Let's deal with him the way the French dealt with Napoleon. Napoleon was dispatched to the island of Elba, where he retained an entourage but was forced to agree never to return to France. The *Politico* writer suggests Trump could similarly be dispatched to the Bikini Atoll in the Marshall Islands, even more distant than Elba, but with a tropical climate that "might remind him of Mar-a-Lago." Again, at the beginning of this year, we have Kirk Swearingen writing in *Salon*, "Can we send Trump into exile? It worked (sort of) with Napoleon." Same idea.[76]

But Trump rejected this easy path, in effect saying, "Bring it on." And so they brought it on. Let's start with Trump's two civil cases, the E. Jean Carroll rape case and Trump's real estate valuation case before Judge Arthur Engoron. The Carroll case was brought as a defamation claim, because Trump denied having sex with Carroll, exposed her kooky personality and snubbed her by saying she wasn't his type. But of course there would be no defamation had Carroll falsely accused Trump of rape, because then he would be a man merely defending himself against her defamation of him. If he did rape her, on the other hand, he'd be adding insult to injury by denigrating her, in a sense victimizing her twice over.

But the very idea that Trump raped Carroll in the Bergdorf Goodman dressing room was, on the face of it, preposterous. The charge itself was ancient, and the statute of limitations had passed. In my interview with her for the film, Trump's lawyer Alina Habba reminded me that Carroll's attorney had worked closely with the New York attorney general Letitia James to pass a new law through the state's Democrat-controlled legislature giving additional time for cases like this to be brought. And as soon as the new law passed, the case was filed. With a manipulative New York judge and a pliant jury largely made up of people politically hostile to Trump, he was found guilty, not of rape, but of having assaulted Carroll and also having defamed her. Trump got a hefty fine of $83.3 million, which he is now appealing.

Next, Trump was charged in New York with business fraud on

the grounds that he grossly inflated the value of his real estate hold-ings when he applied for loans with New York banks. For example, Trump had listed his Palm Beach Mar-a-Lago estate as worth hun-dreds of millions of dollars while the tax appraisals of the property had it valued at a range of $18-28 million. But of course in a hot real estate market like Palm Beach, the market value of properties bears virtually no resemblance to their tax valuations. In the case of Mar-a-Lago, the tax valuation is based on the operating revenue of the club, not the property's resale value. A year or so ago, Debbie and I stayed for a few days at an oceanfront Palm Beach property owned by a friend; this decent but modest three-bedroom home was listed at Zillow for $11 million. The friend owned a beautiful adjoining estate which had a market value of $40-50 million.

Even this property was nothing like Mar-a-Lago, which is an historic landmark. Debbie and I, and our family, have been there multiple times; in fact, we have had two movie premieres there in the magnificent gold-leaf main ballroom. The main building, which resembles a Moorish castle, is 62,500 square feet and has 58 bed-rooms, 33 bathrooms, and sprawls across 17 acres of prime water-front property with a private beach. Any real estate agent will tell you Mar-a-Lago is worth upwards of $500 million and possibly more than a billion dollars. In reality, Trump might have under-val-ued the property.

But of course the judge went with the tax valuation, and con-cluded Trump had lied to the banks about what this property, and his other properties, were worth. Never mind that the banks made their own evaluations, and senior representatives of Deutsche Bank testified that they would happily do the same transaction with Trump again.[77] Never mind that Trump paid back all his loans in full, with interest, and there were no complaints from any banks claiming to have been victimized by any kind of fraud. Judge Engoron said that

Trump committed tax fraud even in the absence of any victims of that fraud. New York state, apparently, was the victim! Once again, Trump got a crippling financial penalty, which he is appealing, but he had to put up a $175 million bond pending the outcome of that appeal.

These injustices, which by themselves would have finished off anyone who is not a billionaire, were just the prelude to the Colorado case which involved tossing Trump off the state's presidential ballot, and the criminal cases, which were filed in rapid succession. For some Democrats, the cases merely reflect Trump's bad character and habitual criminality. But if so, why did he have a clean record until now, and why were all the cases filed in the months leading up to Trump seeking election for a second time? Had Trump faced a single case—say the claim that he held on to classified documents when he should have turned them all in—it would still be unprecedented to charge a former President in this way, but we could examine the case on its merits. But ninety-one criminal charges! In multiple jurisdictions! And every single one of them filed by Democratic prosecutors, mostly in front of Democrat-appointed judges, and all in close coordination with a Democratic White House, occupied by Trump's presumptive 2024 opponent!

The Colorado case came before the Supreme Court because the Secretary of State had ruled, after a short hearing with no due process rights for Trump, that Trump had supported an insurrection against the US government on January 6, 2021, disqualifying him from appearing as a future presidential candidate on the Colorado ballot. Right away we see why the Democrats had been so insistent from the time the January 6 protesters entered the Capitol, that the protest be labeled an "insurrection."

At first, that term seemed to come out of nowhere, and it seemed absurdly out of place. How ridiculous to compare a protest involving no weapons inside the Capitol, and in which the only people who died were Trump supporters killed by police officers as an "insurrection." How preposterous to compare it with heavily-armed Confederate troops moving against the nation's Capitol. But if this characterization of January 6 made no sense, it was legally essential. How else to trigger Section 3 of the Fourteenth Amendment to the Constitution?

Colorado's action was intended as the first salvo in a blue-state juggernaut to expel Trump from the ballot, making his nationwide candidacy unviable, and likely forcing the Republican Party to go with a different candidate. So if Colorado were permitted to get rid of Trump, Maine and Hawaii stood ready to follow suit. Thus Trump was facing the prospect of running for president without being on the ballot of all fifty states. The last time something like this happened, it happened to Lincoln, whose name in the 1860 presidential election did not appear on the ballot of ten Southern states.

The Left and the Democrats were exultant about the prospects of Colorado succeeding, and confident that the Supreme Court would go along. Never Trump Republican judge J. Michel Luttig and left-wing Harvard law professor Laurence Tribe co-authored an article in *The Atlantic* titled, "The Constitution Prohibits Trump From Ever Being President Again." The authors insisted that Section 3 of the Fourteenth Amendment was "self-executing," which would mean that Trump was already disqualified and Colorado and other states were not so much rejecting him as merely recognizing his ineligibility.[78]

The language of the relevant constitutional provision, however, does not support Luttig's and Tribe's reading, or perhaps I should say misreading. Rather, it gives Congress the power to decide who is an insurrectionist, and whether or not that person should be excluded from seeking high office in the future. Consequently, the Supreme Court ruled 9-0 in Trump's favor. I think even the progressives on the Court went along, not because of their regard for the Constitutional text—they have shown no previous fidelity to the actual language of the text—but rather because they feared that if blue states could throw Trump off the ballot, then red states would throw the Democratic nominee off their ballot, and the result would be utter chaos. Prudence, rather than precise constitutional reasoning, produced the unanimous verdict, which predictably drew a crybaby lament from Luttig and Tribe, who followed up with a lachrymose screed, "Supreme Betrayal: A Requiem for Section 3 of the Fourteenth Amendment."[79]

Now we turn to the Fani Willis case in Georgia. Here we have the Fulton County District Attorney attempting to prosecute Trump and a whole cohort of co-defendants for collectively attempting to overturn the 2020 election results in Georgia. Supposedly this group tried to do this by appointing "fake electors" who were intended to supplant the "real electors" representing Biden and Harris who won the state of Georgia. But of course Trump and his team were contesting the Georgia results. What if sufficient fraud were shown that caused the election results to be overturned and the state handed over to Trump? Then it would have been legally necessary for Trump to have his own slate of electors, and the so-called fake electors were actually named to take into account this possibility. In reality they were provisional, not fake, electors.

So there is no crime here, and moreover, Trump himself had nothing to do with the alternate elector slate. What Trump did do was to make a phone call to the Georgia Secretary of State, Brad Raffensperger. According to the criminal indictment, and also countless media reports, Trump in his call demanded that Raffensperger, a fellow Republican, "find" an additional 11,780 votes. The implication is that Trump knew he lost Georgia, but he nevertheless wanted to "find" more votes than he actually got. In other words, Trump was asking Raffensperger to cheat on his behalf.

A simple review of the transcript of the call, however, totally dispels this theory. Trump begins by telling Raffensperger, "We have won this election in Georgia." He repeats this claim multiple times. "We won the election, and it's not fair to take it away from us like this." Indeed, the whole basis of Trump's grievance is that Georgia is moving ahead with faulty results. "Under law," Trump tells Raffensperger, "you're not allowed to give faulty election results. OK? You're not allowed to do that, and that's what you've done." Trump gets to what he wants. "I think you have to say that you're going to re-examine it, and you can re-examine it, but re-examine it with people that want to find answers, not people that don't want to find answers."[80]

Can anything more benign and reasonable be imagined here? Trump firmly believes he won Georgia, and regardless of whether he's right about that or not, he wants a proper inquiry, giving the state to the rightful winner. Trump's phrase, "I just want to find 11,780 votes" must be read against that essential context. Nowhere does Trump say, or even imply, that he wants Raffensperger to produce fraudulent votes on his behalf. I go through all this, because the Fani Willis case has been sidetracked by her extracurricular improprieties, such as naming as lead prosecutor on the case a man she is having an affair with, and then funneling large amounts of money to that man, so that the two of them could go on extravagant trips together. This seeming misconduct might eventually get Willis thrown off the case—which the appellate court will decide after the election—but the point is that even had the case proceeded, it never had any merit. There simply isn't any there there.

Next we turn to the classified documents case, the one that

involved the FBI Mar-a-Lago raid, and here we see that the Biden DOJ had problems from the start. The raid itself was utterly outrageous—no president has ever been raided in that way—and the outrage was compounded by the FBI giving its agents a "use lethal force if necessary" instruction. Yes, the instruction is standard for FBI raids, but the whole point is that this was not a standard FBI raid. The FBI was not raiding, as it typically does, some suspected murderer or drug dealer or terrorist. This was the former president of the United States, and the leading candidate for the GOP nomination in 2024. Moreover, Mar-a-Lago is under Secret Service protection. Not only does this help guarantee the safety of any classified documents stored there—in a padlocked storage room, incidentally—but consider the risks of giving a "lethal force" order to armed FBI agents confronting armed Secret Service agents entrusted with protecting Trump, his family and his residence. At the very least, the Biden regime used extreme recklessness in the way they went about it.

"I was sitting with the president when the raid was happening," Trump's lawyer Alina Habba told me. "We were in New York at Trump Tower." Habba says that Trump was extremely calm, which she said is not indicative of someone who has done something wrong. He wasn't freaked out because "he knew exactly what this was." Lara Trump makes a similar point about Trump's temperament in these situations. "It's like when you're on an airplane and you hit some turbulence, everybody looks immediately at the flight attendant. And if the flight attendants are calm and collected, you're like, okay, well I guess there's nothing to worry about. It's a similar thing with my father-in-law. Even in private, even in moments when I'm expecting him to say, I just wish I hadn't come back in this fight, I have never heard him say that."

While the special counsel, Jack Smith, and the Democrats had pinned high hopes on the classified documents case, their real problem was with the judge. This time they didn't have a compliant Democrat appointee to the bench, someone who would mindlessly go along with the government's prosecutorial scheme. This time they had to contend with the Trump-appointed judge, Aileen Cannon, who showed from the outset that she was fully attuned to at least this aspect of the "get Trump" scheme.

Cannon gave short shrift to the legal pundits, mostly from the Left but also some Never Trump pontificators, who said the classified documents case was a slam dunk for the prosecution—its best chance to nail Trump. Cannon recognized that while Trump had classified documents in his possession, so did other previous Presidents. Mike Pence had classified documents. So did Biden. Biden's secret documents went back to his days as a senator; how he extracted those documents and retained them remains something of a mystery. Biden's classified documents from his tenure as vice president were strewn all over the place: his garage, his residence, the Penn Biden Center. Moreover, Trump as president had the authority to declassify documents and also to retain documents; Biden as vice president did not.

So Judge Cannon had ample legal justification to throw the case out on the basis of selective and vindictive prosecution. Justice, after all, isn't simply a matter of asking, "Did Trump do this?" It's also a matter of asking, "Why haven't all the other presidents and vice presidents who did the same, or worse, not get raided, charged, or prosecuted in any way?" Even so, Judge Cannon found a way to throw out the case that was even more insulting to the Biden DOJ and Special Prosecutor Jack Smith. She dismissed the case on the basis that Smith wasn't even a legitimate special prosecutor. His appointment was unconstitutional! The Constitution requires that special prosecutors be officers of the government, and Jack Smith, who was picked for the job out of private practice by Attorney

General Merrick Garland, wasn't a federal officer, however that term could be construed. In sum, he was an impostor posing as a special counsel. He had to go, and the case had to go!

Next, the January 6 case. This too is a case that is being prosecuted by "Special Counsel" Jack Smith. He remains special counsel in DC until a federal court or the Supreme Court steps in to throw out his appointment there too. But maybe it won't have to, because Jack Smith's far-fetched attempt to show that Trump orchestrated an attempt to overthrow the results of the 2020 election never seems to have gotten off the ground. Leave aside the merit—or perhaps I should say lack of merit—of the charges. Trump never asked anyone to go inside the US Capitol, so there is simply no way to show he meant to stop the proceedings. But of course Jack Smith always knew that. He was counting on a Trump-hating judge, Tanya Chutkan, and a Trump-hating jury to ignore the facts and simply rule that Trump is guilty no matter what.

Enter the US Supreme Court. The Court delivered two body blows to Jack Smith's case, one more devastating than the other. The first was to dismiss the charge that Trump or any of his co-defendants could be charged with "obstructing an official proceeding" absent proof that they actually attempted to alter documents or records of that proceeding. Merely marching into the Capitol and shouting slogans was not enough! (Indeed progressive activists have marched into government buildings, occupied them, and disrupted proceedings on numerous occasions.) The Court said that the law passed in the aftermath of the Enron case, which the Biden DOJ had been using to inflict felony charges on January 6 protesters, and sought to use against Trump, was being misused to cover circumstances remote from what Congress intended when it passed that law. Strike one!

Then the Supreme Court, in a powerful and much-anticipated

decision on presidential immunity, basically ruled that Trump
had presidential immunity and could not be criminally charged
for actions undertaken as part of his official duties. This ruling
involved some nuance, in that the Court distinguished between
the President's core duties, for which he had absolute immunity,
and other actions carried out as part of his office, for which he had
presumptive immunity. But then the Court defined presumptive
immunity—in effect, giving Trump the benefit of the doubt—in
such a way that Trump's actions on January 6 seem largely invul-
nerable to criminal prosecution. Trump, the Court ruled, is only
criminally liable for his personal actions unrelated to his official acts
in office. Strike two!

The howls of rage from the Left and the Democrats following
these Supreme Court rulings were quite amusing to behold. I chuckled every time I read an article saying that Trump's own appointed
judges were letting him off the hook. One might expect me to deny
that this is the case, and to make a lofty argument for the philosophical independence of every justice on the Court. But of course
we all know that justices can be overtly political, and even those
who are not have philosophical or jurisprudential inclinations that
tilt Left or tilt Right. That's why Republicans appoint justices like
Clarence Thomas, Neil Gorsuch and Samuel Alito, and Democrats
appoint justices like Elena Kagan, Sonia Sotomayor and Ketanji
Brown Jackson.

The Democrats understand the politicization of the judiciary,
which is why they are careful to find favorable jurisdictions to file
criminal cases against Trump and his allies. They count on left-
wing judges to get Trump. And therefore Trump doesn't have to
apologize for appointing justices that help him to get out of these
attempted legal assassinations. Trump's judges are merely there to
undo the vicious handiwork of the progressive judges on the lower

and appellate courts. While many Republicans deplore the politicization of the judiciary, and give pompous sermons on the need to
depoliticize the Court, Trump understands that the Court, like the
other branches of government, are basically engaged in an exercise of
power. It's important to repel a power move against your side with
some power moves of your own.

Finally, in our review of the ruthless lawfare against Trump, let's
consider the one case in which the Democrats got the guilty verdict
they had been hoping to get in multiple cases. Here Judge Juan
Merchan, working in close coordination with the New York prosecutors, got a jury to render thirty-four counts of guilty, but only
because he pulled a circus act unheard of in the annals of American
law. Basically, he told the jury that they could find Trump guilty
of misrepresentation, because his company classified as "legal" payments that were admittedly made to a lawyer, but with the intention
of those payments ultimately going to Stormy Daniels in exchange
for her NDA.

This crime, which hardly seems like a crime, is nevertheless only
a misdemeanor. So Merchan found a way to elevate a trivial offense
into a felony. He told the jury that it could find that Trump's purpose in concealing the payment to Daniels was to suppress negative
stories about him at a time when he was running for president. But
wait! What's wrong with that? Well, said Judge Merchan, if you're
going to try and protect your image as a political candidate, that's a
campaign expense. So Trump should have used campaign money to
pay for the NDA. But since he used his personal money, he had run
afoul of federal campaign finance laws.

But again, Trump had never been charged with violating federal
campaign finance laws. In fact, the DOJ had reviewed the situation and declined to charge him. So how could Trump be charged
in a local jurisdiction, New York, with violating federal campaign

finance laws that fall outside the purview of Judge Merchan? Here Judge Merchan instructed the jury that Trump didn't actually have to violate any laws; he merely had to intend to violate them. He could be found guilty based on his presumed state of mind. Finally, if the jury had any confusion or doubts about any of this, they didn't have to agree on what law Trump had violated; they could choose among various violations, and all that mattered was that they all agreed he had violated some law or the other!

If this seems like banana republic stuff, it is. By way of comparison, let's recall that it was the Hillary Clinton campaign that devised the whole Russia collusion hoax. For what purpose? They did so to produce media stories that would portray Trump as a Russian asset, someone in league with Putin, a traitor to the United States. This would then cause many Americans not to vote for Trump, and to vote instead for Hillary. So Russia collusion was from the beginning an election interference scheme. It was an attempt to influence through deception the outcome of the 2016 presidential election. Yet the Hillary campaign disguised its funding of the project—of the notorious Steele dossier—by marking the expense as "legal." They used the exact same designation that Trump used in the Stormy Daniels matter. Yet Hillary was never charged. She was never prosecuted. Instead, her campaign paid a trivial $8,000 fine for misrepresenting payments it made for the Steele dossier.[81] Putting the Trump and Hillary cases side-by-side, we can see the serious problem we have in this country in the way the law is selectively deployed against one person and not another, against one party and not the other one.

Even so, the jury saluted the corrupt scheme jointly cooked up by New York prosecutors and Judge Merchan, and the Democrats got their headlines the next day. Guilty! Guilty on all thirty-four counts! (It was thirty-four counts because Trump's lawyer made thirty-four installment payments and each was treated as a separate felony.)

Consider this jubilant post from Alex Soros, the son of George Soros and in many people's estimation, an even bigger monster than his notorious father. "Democrats," he wrote, "should refer to Trump as a convicted felon at every opportunity. Repetition is the key to a successful message and we want people to wrestle with the notion of hiring a convicted felon for the most important job in the country!"[82] Here Soros candidly admits what the Democrats were going for in all their cases.

But, incredibly, it didn't work. Trump's poll numbers went up. In other words, the American people seem to have wrestled with the notion of hiring a convicted felon for the most important job in the country and come to the conclusion that this particular one would be just fine. For those who are disturbed at the very idea, let's remember that Martin Luther King Jr, Nelson Mandela, Mahatma Gandhi, and Aleksandr Solzhenitsyn were all convicts. Did this mean they were untrustworthy and no one ought to have hired them or named them to any responsible post?

Of course not. When the system itself is unjust—or when the system is being deployed in a manifestly unjust way—the heroes are the ones with felony convictions. The good guys are the ones in the prison uniforms! And in Trump's case, the reason for his boost in public support was that many people saw through the Democrats' lawfare scheme. They understood that Trump was only being prosecuted in this case, as he was prosecuted in the real estate evaluation case and the classified documents case, because he was Trump. If the same thing had been done by anyone other than Trump, there would be no prosecution. This is the very definition of the abuse of law—the very lawlessness Lincoln warned against in his Lyceum speech.

The genius of Trump in this situation is to not merely to have done his characteristic rope-a-dope and avoided the worst blows his legal assailants attempted to land on him, but also to then launch a counterattack of his own, putting the Biden DOJ and the local Democrat prosecutors like Alvin Bragg and Fani Willis on trial themselves. Trump's lawyer Alina Habba told me that Trump is actively involved in the legal cases, working closely with his legal team to develop arguments and strategies. Trump fully understands, she said, that these cases aren't strictly legal but are part of a political strategy to torpedo his chances in the 2024 election. Through a systematic and sustained public expose of these thugs with badges—combined with some shrewd legal maneuvering to win some of the cases, cripple others, and coolly punt still others beyond the election—Trump achieved what no one inside or outside the legal profession would have thought possible, or at least practicable. Trump achieved Megyn Kelly's inside straight, and he did it himself, on his own strength, and by and large without the public support of the GOP.

Now let's proceed from character assassination and legal assassination to actual assassination. Let's begin by noting that Trump's security—which is to say, his life—is in the hands of his political opponents. Why? Because the Secret Service tasked with protecting Trump is part of the Department of Homeland Security. The secret service director reports to DHS Secretary Alejandro Mayorkas. Mayorkas is a stooge of the Biden-Harris regime. Now in the past, this dependency of a candidate of one party on the executive branch controlled by the other party was not really a problem. But now, in the wake of the things the Biden regime has tried to do to Trump, his reliance on them for his personal security has become a serious issue.

The Biden regime has the motive, the means, and the opportunity to permanently get rid of Trump. The motive could not be stronger: to be rid once and for all of a massively dangerous opponent that they have been trying to eliminate in other ways—in fact, every way they can. The Biden regime was also in charge of security for the area where Trump spoke in Butler, Pennsylvania. Finally, there is the question of opportunity. I am not suggesting that there was a plan worked out in the White House or at DHS to assassinate Trump, and that the shooter was recruited for this purpose. Not at all. A conspiracy so elaborate is not believable, not because it is a "conspiracy theory" (dismissing something as a conspiracy theory only works if conspiracies don't exist), but rather because it would surely have been found out. Someone in the system—possibly a Secret Service agent or agents loyal to Trump—would have blown the whistle. No, it didn't go down like that. I'm not sure exactly how it went down.

What I do know is that there was too much incompetence for the incompetence theory to be credible. Is it really believable that the young shooter had a drone and the Secret Service didn't? Or that the man was able to fire multiple shots from a nearby roof without that roof having agents up there? Is Secret Service Director Kim Cheatle's claim that they didn't put agents up on the roof because it had a slope and they might fall even remotely credible? Why didn't the authorities, on being informed by rallygoers that there was a man with a gun on the roof, remove Trump from the stage? Without going into every detail of supposed incompetence, we can simply ask the question: How does a twenty-year-old Gen Z kid outsmart the Secret Service? The answer, of course, is that he doesn't.

For this reason, I think the assassination attempt was partly an inside job. Here's how I think it could have gone down. The intelligence agencies of the government, which are basically instruments of the Biden regime, discover that there are a few lunatics out there who would like to take out former President Trump. Conceivably they even know about this guy Crooks. They know what he's planning, and someone very high up in the Secret Service decides: we're just going to let him do it. We're going to look the other way until he makes the attempt, and then once the deed is done we'll quickly take him out. Since dead men tell no tales, no one will ever figure out that we enabled this to happen, and even if there is massive fallout regarding the "negligence" of the Secret Service, that can be fixed with a couple of high-profile resignations and pledges to do better in the future. A small price to pay for putting Trump in a casket!

Further investigation—if we can even rely on this being carried out in an honest way—will have to reveal the full story of the assassination attempt, which was not meant to fail and, applying the familiar laws of probability, should not have failed. Hitting a target from a short distance away with an AR-15 is ridiculously easy. Debbie and I have shot AR-15s at the shooting range. It's basically impossible to miss! And the shooter had Trump in his sights.

Yet he missed. The scene is reminiscent of the movie *The Day of the Jackal*, in which a highly-capable assassin aims accurately and fires a single shot at the French president Charles de Gaulle. He misses, but only because at that very second, de Gaulle leans forward to kiss a French soldier on the cheek. In virtually the same way, Trump turned his head slightly to look at a large screen with some illegal immigration numbers on it, and the bullet that would have gone through his brain missed and merely grazed him on the cheek. The cartoonist Scott Adams posted on X that Trump's narrow escape may have been a case of "God doing early voting" and, I have to say, that's as good an explanation as any.[83]

Even so, Trump's face was splattered with blood. According to Trump, he felt a sharp pain that was similar, as he told Robert F. Kennedy Jr. in a phone call, to being stung by a "giant mosquito."[84] Other shots sounded, and Trump was swamped by Secret Service agents who dragged him down, pummeling his body so hard that his shoes flew off. What happened next, however, was legendary. Trump drew himself back up, raised his fist, and shouted "Fight, fight, fight." Obviously, there was no way for Trump to rehearse this or put it on; it was his natural and instinctive reaction. Moreover, it occurred in full public view and was recorded on video and immortalized in a journalist's photograph. Eerily the photograph reminded one of the famous Iwo Jima photograph from the World War II era. Trump, in a single moment, joined the panorama of history and, through his demonstration of unparalleled strength and bravery, made history.

Stunned at Trump's display of character under the most trying circumstance, the Democrats and the Left quickly moved to downplay and re-interpret the incident. Many newspaper headlines refused to use the term "assassination." Other sources denied that Trump had even been shot. Several pundits speculated that perhaps Trump had been struck by a piece of shrapnel, even though there is an actual photo of the bullet whizzing toward Trump's head. My old friend David Frum—now an incorrigible Never Trumper—published a long article in the *Atlantic* arguing that Trump himself was to blame because he had fomented an atmosphere of violence.[85] By this logic, Lincoln was to blame for his own assassination, because Lincoln created the environment that caused John Wilkes Booth to do what he did. Even the Democrats of the Confederacy didn't have the indecency to make that claim. Frum's shameless piece, a classic instance of "blaming the victim," shows the moral sickness of our public discourse. This is what Trump has to deal with: someone tries to assassinate him, and his critics say he brought it on himself.

When I interviewed Trump at Mar-a-Lago, I reminded him of his interview with Charlie Rose in the early 1990s. When Rose asked Trump what he was most proud about, Trump had answered he was most proud of the fact that, in economically treacherous times, he had survived. But it wasn't just the fact he had survived; it was the way he had survived. And I told Trump that the same could be said about the attempted assassination. It wasn't just that Trump survived it; it was the way he survived that revealed an inner dimension that could not be denied.

Is there any moment in US history that compares with this? I can think of only one. When Teddy Roosevelt was giving a campaign speech in Milwaukee in 1912, a would-be assassin put a bullet in him. Roosevelt continued speaking! It was only when someone challenged him that he announced that he had been shot, adding however that it took more than a single bullet to stop a Bull Moose.[86] Roosevelt at this time was fifty-four years old; Trump is seventy-eight. And quite astonishingly, Trump shows no signs of paranoia or PTSD following the incident; he resumed his rallies almost immediately, and even returned to Butler, Pennsylvania to do another rally there—a typical Trumpian gesture of defiance.

I'd like to conclude this chapter with what Aristotle says about courage, because I think it helps illuminate the magnitude and the precise nature of what Trump has shown throughout his career, but especially in response to the assassination attempt. I'm drawing here on political scientist Lorraine Pangle's essay, "The Anatomy of Courage in Aristotle's *Nicomachean Ethics*," published in the *Review of Politics*.[87] Aristotle insists that courage is the greatest virtue, because it enables all the others. This is an important enough point, but Aristotle goes on to make a second one that is, in my view, even more crucial.

Aristotle denies that common view that courage means fearlessness or overcoming fear. Aristotle argues that the person who has truly overcome fear is the reckless person. A man who fearlessly dives off a precipice is not to be admired! But neither, says Aristotle, is the man to be admired who will never go near a precipice. The man who avoids danger at all costs is a timid or cowardly man. Thus, Aristotle says, applying his famous doctrine of the mean, courage is the virtue that is intermediate between the extremes of recklessness and cowardice. The courageous man feels fear, but pushes forward nevertheless, because there is a worthy goal ahead and the risk is one that is worth taking.

In Pangle's account of Aristotle, courage is a complex virtue which cannot be reduced to the intellect alone. Rather, courage involves intelligent evaluation, a prudent willingness to endure fear, and finally action that is taken with an understanding of the dangers and risks involved. Trump, in an episode that will forever encapsulate his true character, proved on that fateful day in Butler, Pennsylvania that if America wants and needs a wartime general for these parlous times, he's our man.

CHAPTER 6

THE BALLOT MAKERS

_____

I consider it completely unimportant who will vote, or how; but what is important is who will count the votes.[88]

—Joseph Stalin

How so you solve a problem like Donald Trump? Everything the Left and the Democrats have thrown at him, he has so far thwarted and overcome. Against all odds, Trump has endured and, to a considerable degree, even prevailed. The guy literally dodged a bullet! So now what? There is only one thing to do, a sort of Democratic final solution. That solution is to cheat. We should pause here to see how cheating in an election is precisely the kind of lawlessness that Lincoln warned about in his Lyceum speech. Moreover, the forms of cheating that we will encounter—such as using the names of illegals to cast illicit votes—are themselves reliant on a whole system of lawbreaking that brings the illegals into the country in the first place. Lincoln's call for Americans to recommit ourselves to reverence for the laws seems far-fetched when one of the two major political parties is institutionally committed to cheating its way to victory.

So the question becomes, can the Democrats rig and steal the 2024 election? If they try, is there a way for Trump and his allies to stop them? My answers to these questions is yes. The Democrats are likely to cheat, and to attempt to steal the presidential election. And yes, there is a way—multiple ways—to prevent this from happening and also to bust it while it is happening. But to stop the steal, one has to know where the steal is taking place. Here it's crucial to realize that Democrats don't do the same type of heist every time. If they did, it would be easier to catch them in the act. In 2024, however, they are likely to try some new ways of cheating, knowing that the Trump campaign, patriots, and Republicans will be looking for the old ways.

Therefore, we must be alert not only to the schemes that Democrats have used in the past, but also to vulnerabilities in our election process that give rise to new possibilities for election fraud. Notice that I say election fraud and not voter fraud. There is a difference between the two terms. Voter fraud refers to a voter who is trying to cast an illicit ballot, or perhaps to vote multiple times by casting a ballot in different states. This by itself is not going to change the outcome of any election. But election fraud is organized, coordinated fraud. It is aimed at tipping the election result in favor of one candidate or party over another. In this chapter we're focused on election fraud, not voter fraud.

Let's be clear that the legal cases hurled at Donald Trump in an election year—aimed at locking him up and taking him out of the race—were themselves a brazen form of election interference. Election interference has now become a staple of American politics, and it always comes from the same side. In 2016, the Russia collusion hoax was devised as a form of election interference. In 2020, as we saw in an earlier chapter, Covid was used as the pretext for election interference. Fauci and Walensky's bogus six feet rule became a justification for the proliferation of mail-in dropboxes, a convenient way to dump large numbers of illicit ballots into unsupervised collection facilities.

Election interference is a form of cheating. We also know that

In his Lyceum Address, a young Abraham Lincoln warned of the danger of a tyrant or dictator who would rise to power in America and subvert our constitutional republic. Today the threat of dictatorship is real, but which side does it come from? *(Public Domain)*

Donald Trump at a fairly young age became both an entrepreneurial titan and a major cultural celebrity. Given that he is a man of larger-than-life dimensions and power, the Left and the Democrats naturally accused him of aspiring to be a dictator. *(Getty Images)*

George Orwell, author of the classic works Animal Farm and 1984, spelled out the characteristic features of a tyrannical society which include mass surveillance, widespread censorship, ideological propaganda, and criminalization of political differences. *(Public Domain)*

Aleksandr Solzhenitsyn, author of The Gulag Archipelago, warned that Soviet-style tyranny might look somewhat different in other countries but could happen anywhere. Its hallmark, he wrote, is the corruption of the justice system and the promotion of lawlessness under the guise of law. *(Getty Images)*

This is the fateful moment in which Obama, with smiling reluctance, turned over the leadership of the country to Trump. Obama failed to mention, of course, that he had been working with the intelligence agencies to frame Trump as a Russian spy and an asset of Vladimir Putin. *(Getty Images)*

My family's first meeting with Donald Trump in the Oval Office in November 2019. I am sitting in the "dictator's chair." On the Left are my wife Debbie and my stepson Justin Fancher. On the right are my daughter Danielle and her husband Brandon Gill. *(Courtesy of the author)*

Posing with Trump for a group photo following our conversation with the President. *(Courtesy of the author)*

Trump shakes hands with my son-in-law Brandon Gill. Thanks to a Trump endorsement, Brandon won his Republican primary in Texas #26, a red, pro-Trump district in the suburbs of Dallas. If all goes well in November, he will be a Congressman next year. *(Courtesy of the author)*

Close-up of Trump immediately following the assassination attempt. Trump's instinctive reaction to being shot provides a classic illustration of his natural bravery and courage, just one of a long list of Trump virtues that his critics never mention. *(Getty Images)*

It's hard to see tyranny represented by "cackling Kamala" and "shuffling Biden." But modern tyranny is typically carried out by a political party and a regime, and figures like Biden and Harris are sometimes just front-men or apparatchiks of the regime that directs and controls them. *(Getty Images)*

Trump arrives at the Mar-a-Lago grand ballroom for the red-carpet premiere of *2000 Mules*. *(Courtesy of the author)*

Trump getting ready to sit down and watch *2000 Mules* at the red-carpet premiere. *(Courtesy of the author)*

Trump praised *2000 Mules* for substantiating his claims that the 2020 election was rigged and stolen. At the very least, the film conclusively debunked the canard that that election was "the most secure election in US history." *(Courtesy of the author)*

Trump watches *2000 Mules* and provides a running commentary, including such gems as praising me for my "movie voice" and explaining what I might have been forced to do if I didn't have such a voice. *(Courtesy of the author)*

Silhouette of Trump, me and my wife Debbie watching the film at the premiere. *(Courtesy of the author)*

Debbie and I pose with Trump, who, as I spell out in this book, is a very different man up close from his public image. *(Courtesy of the author)*

Debbie and I are all smiles with Trump. This photo was taken in July 2024 when I interviewed Trump for the movie *Vindicating Trump*. *(Courtesy of the author)*

Trump's lawyer Alina Habba and I strike a genial pose following our serious conversation about the "legal assassination" being attempted through Trump's 91 criminal cases. *(Courtesy of the author)*

Prior to my interview with Lara Trump, we took a short ride on a golf cart at the Trump Golf property in Westchester, New York. *(Courtesy of the author)*

This photo was taken during my conversation with Alina Habba about Trump's criminal cases, an attempt, as she described it, to permanently silence Trump's powerful voice. *(Courtesy of the author)*

This photo was taken during my conversation with Lara Trump, who confessed her astonishment at our revelation, in this book and the accompanying movie, that ballots can with relative ease by bought and made in this country, greatly increasing the opportunities for election fraud. *(Courtesy of the author)*

Our film crew strikes a final note before I begin my conversation with Donald Trump which can be seen in the movie and read in the Afterword to this book. *(Courtesy of the author)*

My interview with Donald Trump, conducted just a few days after the assassination attempt and the Republican National Convention, had a different beat and tone than many other interviews Trump has given. How so? Well, you'll just have to see for yourself. *(Courtesy of the author)*

The artist Jon McNaughton did this striking portrait of Candace Owens, Trump and me. You also might notice a familiar figure groveling on the ground. *(Illustration courtesy of Jon McNaughton)*

Spotted on a Dallas overpass while *2000 Mules* was playing in theaters nationwide. *(Courtesy of the author)*

A relaxed photo with Trump following my presidential pardon. I didn't know Trump before that, and oddly the pardon set me on a journey of understanding a man who inspires the most intense reactions of love and hate of any American president since Lincoln. *(Courtesy of the author)*

some of the biggest tech platforms—Google, YouTube, Facebook, Instagram—will continue this year to censor pro-Trump content while amplifying anti-Trump content. This is their way of putting their digital thumbs on the scales of the election. This might be a legal form of cheating, but it's cheating nevertheless. That's why you'll never see Google or Facebook boast that they are manipulating their algorithms to favor the Democrats. That's why they do it in secret while pretending that they are being fair and impartial.

My focus in this chapter, however, is on the two new ways in which Democrats might cheat in the 2024 election. The first way is by getting the votes of hundreds of thousands, perhaps millions, of illegals. I am not saying that illegals are rushing to vote; illegals by and large don't care about voting. Rather, I'm talking about ballots cast on behalf of illegals that the illegals themselves are indifferent to or not even aware of. I'm talking about getting the names of illegals on the voter rolls, and then casting ballots on their behalf. The second type of fraud is by making ballots by the thousands, perhaps by the hundreds of thousands, and then filling them out using select names from the voter rolls and dumping these illicit votes into mail-in dropboxes. Although I'm quite well versed on the topic of election fraud, after having made the film *2000 Mules*, I was completely unaware that it's possible to make or create ballots. That's why this chapter is called "The Ballot Makers."

The issue of election fraud has come to the forefront of our politics with the widespread understanding, on the part of a great number of Americans, that the 2020 election was rigged and stolen. This, of course, was heatedly denied by the Democrats and the media, who insisted with tiresome pomposity that on the contrary, that election was "the most secure in American history." But on the face of it that is absurd. Why? Because when has anyone produced a demonstration of any sort showing that the volume of fraud in 2020 was less than in 2016, 2012, 2008 or any previous election? Such a demonstration has never been produced; indeed, it has never even been attempted.

Just a few months after the election, in early 2021, *Time* magazine published the cover story, "The Secret History of the Shadow Campaign that Saved the 2020 Election." Throughout the article, reporter Molly Ball wrote about "saving," "protecting," and "fortifying" the election, but from what? From "Trump's assault on democracy." Yet how can a candidate running for office within a democratic system of elections be assaulting democracy? Quite obviously this was code language for guaranteeing a victory for the Democrats. Ball made it quite clear that the only way to save, protect and fortify democracy in this case was to assure a victory for Joe Biden and Kamala Harris.

Ball did not hesitate to describe the project as a conspiracy. "This is the inside story of the conspiracy to save the 2020 election . . . a well-funded cabal of powerful people, ranging across industries and ideologies, working together behind the scenes to influence perceptions, change rules and laws, steer media coverage and control the flow of information." The actions of the conspirators, Ball continued, "touched every aspect of the election. They got states to change voting systems and laws and helped secure hundreds of millions in public and private funding. They fended off voter-suppression lawsuits, recruited armies of poll workers, and got millions of people to vote by mail for the first time. They successfully pressured social media companies to take a harder line against disinformation and used data-driven strategies to fight vital smears. After Election Day, they monitored every pressure point to ensure that Trump could not overturn the result. They were not rigging the election; they were fortifying it."[89]

Fortifying it? What's the correct term when one side alters voting systems and laws in its favor, deploys huge amounts of private and public funding to achieve its objectives, recruits election supervisors from its own team, installs a new system of massive mail-in voting, works in tandem with digital platforms to censor the opposition's messaging on grounds of "misinformation," and then blocks efforts to review, audit, or even publicly question the election result? This is rigging, not fortification.

The one thing that Ball never mentioned—I get the impression it's the one thing she assiduously avoided—was illegal ballot trafficking. There were numerous references in the *Time* article to getting out the vote—sometimes abbreviated GOTV—and getting people to vote for the first time. There were glowing tributes to GOTV organizations staffed by left-wing activists that sought to increase voter participation in Democratic areas.

Nowhere, however, was there a single reference to mules getting paid to deposit fraudulent ballots in mail-in dropboxes. Election fraud itself was treated as a non-issue. Concerns on the part of Trump or Republicans about election fraud appeared only in the context of "voter suppression." Thus rules that made it easy to cheat became, in Ball's inverted logic, a tool for fighting voter suppression and protecting democracy. What's valuable about Ball's article is not what Ball sought to convey—in fact, it's the very opposition of what she sought to convey. What Ball revealed is how Democrats created an elaborate infrastructure to enable an election heist, even though she made no reference to the heist itself. Evidently the Democrats and the media wanted to boast about how ingeniously and laboriously they rigged the 2020 election without actually admitting they did it. They merely "fortified" it.

In May 2022, I helped to bust the fraud that swung the election to Biden in my documentary film *2000 Mules*. Prior to the release of that film, most of the discussion of election fraud had focused on "anomalies." And of course there were many anomalies, but anomalies are merely puzzles that require explanation. They don't offer sufficient proof of fraud to cast an election outcome into doubt. But *2000 Mules* did provide such proof, or at least it provided powerful evidence that required further investigation to confirm that hundreds of thousands of fraudulent votes had indeed been cast by an elaborate network of leftist organizers, and the fraud was of sufficient magnitude to alter the election outcome.

The power of *2000 Mules* was it made its case using two forms of technology that are entirely reliable and regularly used by the law enforcement agencies of the US government. The research group True the Vote assembled and analyzed this data, and its findings were presented in the movie. I was recently watching a murder case on TV and I heard one of the legal commentators make the point that juries these days are not easily convinced even by eyewitness testimony, because they now know that eyewitnesses can be unreliable. Rather, he said, juries convict based on three types of evidence: DNA, cell phone geotracking, and surveillance video. And indeed two of those types of evidence—cell phone geotracking and surveillance video—formed the basis for the exposé of systematic election fraud in *2000 Mules*.

There is simply no need for me to address silly claims about the movie, such as the claim by several fact checkers, notably Ali Swenson of AP, that geotracking doesn't work reliably.[90] Simply look up the *New York Times* article, "One Nation, Tracked," published in 2019. It uses geolocation data to follow the movements of several people at the White House, the Pentagon, and even Mar-a-Lago. Sample quotation: "A single dot appeared on the screen, representing the precise location of someone in President Trump's entourage at 7:10 a.m. It lingered around the grounds of the President's Mar-a-Lago Club in Palm Beach, Fla., where the president was staying for about an hour . . . The data can see the places you go every moment of the day, whom you meet or spend the night with, where you pray, whether you visit a methadone clinic, a psychiatrist's office or a massage parlor."[91]

I do want to address perhaps the most serious criticism of *2000 Mules* that was made by some skeptics after the movie came out. Where, they asked, is the video footage of the same mule at multiple dropboxes? A reasonable question. And here's my answer. Many states such as Wisconsin didn't do any surveillance video. True the Vote was not able to obtain any footage out of Pennsylvania, even though some might exist. In Michigan, there was very limited footage. In Arizona, the same. In Maricopa County, there were surveillance cameras, but most of them were turned off. Even in Georgia, where True the Vote obtained most of its video, many counties did no surveillance at all. Others said they didn't have it or couldn't provide it. Even in areas where it was provided, only a small percentage of the dropboxes had surveillance video.

So had the states followed the election rules—which call for 24/7 surveillance on all dropboxes—it would have been easy to find mules not just at two or three but at ten or more locations. In fact, we would be able to tell by cell phone geotracking when mules arrived at each destination and then capture them on video in those locations. It is the failure of the states to do their job and install cameras that explains my inability to provide what Ben Shapiro and others wanted.

But let me show, by way of an analogy, why their demand is excessive, and why what I did show in the movie adequately makes the case. Consider a serial killer who has gone in a single night to five homes and killed five different people. Now the question before us is, what evidence would we reasonably demand to be satisfied that he did this? Let's say the suspect's phone places him at each of the five homes at the time of death for each of the victims. Let's also assume that only one of the five homes had video surveillance. This matches my contention that only a small percentage of dropboxes had properly installed surveillance cameras. So we review the suspect's phone, and we can tell from the geotracking that he arrived at home number 3 at 2:15 a.m. We look on the surveillance camera and, sure enough, we can see the guy in that home at precisely that time.

Now along comes a skeptic—serving, let's say, on the jury—who asks, "Where is the video of the guy at the other homes?" The obvious answer is, "We can't show you that video because it doesn't exist. It doesn't exist because those homes didn't have proper video surveillance." Yet if we can establish for sure that the suspect was in fact at those locations—and the cell phone data is sufficient to do that—and moreover, if we can confirm that in the one case where there is video, it corroborates the geotracking, then we have two independent sources of proof beyond a reasonable doubt. Don't we have enough here for a conviction? I think yes.

The Rasmussen Survey polled a representative sample of likely voters, and 77 percent of those who saw *2000 Mules* said the movie strengthened their conviction that there was systematic and widespread fraud in the 2020 election. The movie even persuaded independents and Democrats who had been subjected to nearly two years of sustained propaganda about how the 2020 election was the most secure ever.[92] And the Rasmussen team then did a national telephone survey which revealed that more than 20 percent of voters who used mail-in ballots in 2020 admitted they participated in at least one form of election fraud. Some of these voters said they cast a ballot in a state where they no longer lived; others said they filled out a ballot for a friend or family member. All of these practices are illegal.[93] Suffice to say that the 2020 election was quite likely the least secure election in US history.

In the midterm election of 2022, patriots in Arizona camped out at the mail-in dropboxes with their cell phone cameras at the ready in case any mules showed up. The cheat in Maricopa County, however, took a different form that year. Somehow, on Election Day the tabulating machines in a number of precincts didn't work properly. This created long delays and many voters gave up and didn't vote that day. Since Democrats had urged their voters to do early voting, while Republicans had aimed their efforts at turning out voters on Election Day, it is easy to guess which side was disproportionately affected by the machine malfunction in Maricopa County. County officials later said the glitches were unintentional, but this claim was undercut by the discovery that the paper that goes into the tabulating machines was apparently calibrated to the wrong size. It was calibrated, in other words, not to fit properly into the tabulators.[94] In any event, Republicans suffered losses in Arizona in the gubernatorial race and others they were projected to win.

So what about 2024? In order to expose the vulnerability of our election system, our film team asked a former Project Veritas investigator, Ernest White, to look into new ways in which bad actors might game the system to tip the election their way. White worked with a conservative activist named Rick Weible, a business owner and computer consultant, and the two of them created a demonstration project. They sought to demonstrate that they could buy legitimate ballot paper stock—of the identical type used by states in federal elections—and make ballots. They then attempted to show how these ballots could be printed en masse and then filled out with the names and signatures of voters who would have no idea that someone else was casting ballots on their behalf. Finally they sought to demonstrate that these ballots would be accepted as legitimate by state authorities, and that there was virtually no chance the fraud would be detected.

My interview with White and Weible from the film is so startling and disturbing that I have chosen to present a good bit of it, in the question and answer format, here. The interview is slightly edited for clarity. But this way you get it, not in paraphrase, but "from the horse's mouth." I just wish I could include the video demonstration of these two guys buying ballots, duplicating them, and then verifying with election officials that their fake ballots are kosher.

> **Question:** Rick, you said something I find scandalous. You said, Dinesh, if you want to run for office, here's what you need to do. Don't worry about the voters. They don't need to worry about you. You just need to hire me. So I want to explore this. How would you steer me to a landslide victory?
>
> **Rick Weible:** The reality is, there are so many state laws that give us avenues to buy the ballots, print the ballots, and deliver them to cross the finish line to victory.
>
> **Q:** How do you buy a ballot?
>
> **Weible:** We know the shops that typically make ballots for states and deliver them. These are private companies. And some of them just house ballots for backups so the counties can have them and others actually do the full-service of distributing the absentee ballots for counties, states and cities.
>
> **Q:** Now you and Ernest actually went out and bought ballots.
>
> **Weible:** Sure. You too can call one of these companies and go ahead and place the order. For some of them, you can order online.

Ernest White: I had it shipped right to my house. At first, I didn't believe—I said to myself, there's no way an election can be stolen by simply purchasing ballots or printing ballots. Rick showed me that you can buy the ballot paper and simply go to printing companies—any printing company—and just print them out. You just print out as many ballots as you want.

Q: When you say buy a ballot, do you mean you buy the appropriate paper for the ballot? Then how do you actually get all the information printed on the ballot?

Weible: Easy. You buy the official paper. And then you go to the country or secretary of state's website and you can look up to see exactly what your ballot would look like. Or, if you don't want to use the computer, just go ahead and request an absentee ballot to be sent to your home address and then copy that.

Q: Now is there any marking on the ballot that makes it impossible for that ballot to be duplicated?

Weible: Actually there are no markings on the ballots, no type of barcode that identifies that it is unique, because under federal and state laws you're not supposed to associate a voter with a particular ballot, so any type of code or serial number is not allowed.

Q: So a ballot in this respect is different from, say, a $20 bill, because a $20 bill has a number on there and all kinds of markings that allow a teller to say this is a valid note. But you're saying that's not true of a ballot. So to the degree that ballots are the currency of our democracy, what you're saying is counterfeiting is easy to do.

Weible: It's because we value money more than our actual votes in this country.

Q: Is counterfeiting of the ballot in the manner you describe illegal?

Weible: In most states, no. Because states actually want you to print the sample ballots and even use the ballots to teach your children how to vote. You can even print out ballots so you can do research on each of the candidates.

White: We can actually legally print ballots. I called the Voter Registration Office and said, am I okay? Can I make copies of my ballot? And they put me on hold for about 10 minutes and came back and said, sure you can. You can make as many copies as you want.

Q: So if you have a family, for example, you can run five ballots off the printer, and then turn them in and that's allowed.

White: Oh, yeah. You can do that.

Q: So you can buy ballots, which you guys did, and make copies of them, which you also did.

Weible: We were able to, the first time, purchase 10,000 ballots. We downloaded the ballot information right from the state website. We printed it out. We actually went to the election officials and tested the ballots. They verified that they would be ready by their machines. Then we purchased another 5,000 ballots. We went to a local print shop, and we handed them a flash card. They took the flash drive, and they printed out a thousand ballots for us. No questions asked. And the guy came over and said, how many are you guys going to print? I said, about 5,000. He said, I want you to use my big machine.

Q: Let's say you now have 10,000 ballots. Now my question is, if I want to convert those ballots into votes, how do I do that? Is there any way I find out in my home state who are the people on the voter rolls who, let's say, haven't voted in the last two or three elections?

Weible: Absolutely. Some of those voter rolls from the states are free, and some are available at a low cost. In Wisconsin, it costs $15. In Minnesota, $42. Other states provide them for free.

White: I did that, actually just a few weeks ago. I went to the local registrar's office and filled out a quick application. I got a list of over a million names. It cost me $35. That's every registered voter in that county. Or you can get the whole state.

Q: So I just have to request the voter rolls. I then go down the list and see who hasn't voted. This way if I want to vote somebody else's ballot, I can do that.

Weible: Yes. And so the four places I'm going to look for right away are the colleges where students have already graduated, but they're still registered, and the nursing homes where they haven't removed the dead people from the rolls, and the homeless shelters where people have improved their lives and left but they are still registered to vote.

White: I would do the same things you did, but I would go further. I would put all the names in an Excel spreadsheet, and what I'm going to find are these big gaps. As you're scrolling, you're going to see the big gaps. The gaps mean those people didn't vote in any other election.

Q: Let's take a homeless shelter and let's say there are 300 guys who show up for food. I want to illegally vote all their votes. Now normally this would seem a cumbersome process, because I have to go to them, maybe give them 20 bucks apiece, convince them to request an absentee ballot. Then the ballot has to be mailed to them. Then I have to go back and get those ballots from them, fill them out, maybe give them another 20 bucks each. This is a pain.

Weible: You don't have to do all that. In most states it's not illegal, it's actually recommended, to have the director or someone else at the facility go in and register those voters and then give them ballots and then deliver all those ballots back to the county.

Q: Are you saying the absentee ballot application and the ballot itself can be simultaneously filled in and turned in?

Weible: Yes, we've seen that in multiple jurisdictions.

White: Keeping it simple, though, if you're the caseworker, you're probably enrolling all those people onto the voter rolls already. I talked to many homeless people, and they all said they were registered by their caseworker. So now the ballots are going to come to that shelter. I could have 500 ballots coming to that shelter. And maybe 200 of the homeless people actually come get their ballots. What happens to the other 300 ballots? They are up for grabs. If you're that type of person, you could just fill those out and put those in.

Q: How would you round up votes on a college campus?

Weible: In many states they're now passing laws requiring the Secretary of State to collect the names of all the students registered at the schools and allowing them to be registered automatically at the precincts of the school. This creates an opportunity where the students are unaware they are now registered at these campuses. So bad actors can potentially inject ballots on their behalf.

Q: A student could live in one state, but then go to school in another, say Arizona. Suddenly they're registered in Arizona. And if somebody voted using their name in Arizona, they wouldn't know about it.

Weible: That's right. Most voters don't go check their voter history to find out if they voted in another state, or even the state they live in.

Q: Many Americans move from one state to another in the course of their lives. I've lived in seven states over the past 30 years. Is there a way to know someone has moved, but their name is still on the voter rolls?

Weible: We have access to the National Change of Address, which is done by the US Post Office. It allows us do a three year look back. So we can run that against the voter rolls and see who's moved, but the Secretary of State hasn't removed them from the voter rolls.

Q: When I move, I noticed that everybody else knows, like the DMV, the tax authority, they all know. Multiple federal and state agencies are on top of this, which means they have the capacity to track it very easily. But a notable exception are the voter people, who don't track it very well, if they track it at all. It's as if these other agencies don't notify the election office, and the election office doesn't really care.

White: Most of those other agencies will say it's not their job to do this.

Q: Okay, so I now have my ballots and I fill them out using these names off the voter rolls. How do I get them delivered?

Weible: A lot of the dropboxes throughout the United States, they're unsecured. There's no video recording. So it's completely open to drop in as many as you want.

Q: What about signature matching? What kind of signature matching is going on?

Weible: Very little to none. They may just be reviewing the signature on the application and the envelope, which is probably the same person that did those.

Q: What you're saying is that if there's a cheater, he obviously signed both the application and the ballot envelope.

Weible: More than likely. Yeah.

White: The person doing the signature matching, this is the person making minimum wage. And I've got to go through thousands of signatures. So guess what I'm doing. Click, click, click, click.

Weible: Some states don't do matching at all, but even in states that do, these are people who are untrained, who are not evaluating signatures at a professional level, because they are our neighbors that are sitting there trying to do this. And if were to try, we could barely do it ourselves. We might look at a few, but after a while we're going to get tired and just cave to the process.

Q: What's this I hear about vouching for a full van of voters who have not been seen to step outside the van or produce any identification whatsoever?

White: In states like Minnesota, they have a policy where you can vouch for up to eight people. Those people don't have to have any ID or proof of where they live. A registered voter can vouch for these eight people.

Q: Even if they're illegal? My family members from India are not eligible for vote. If they're in my van, can I vouch for them?

White: All they have to do typically is check a box saying they're eligible to vote, and that's it. They're done. They're all set.

Q: No one asks for any documentation? They don't have to produce a passport or anything like that?

White: No. If your relatives come here from India, during voting season we just go to Minnesota and all eight of them can vote.

Weible: If you're a professional voucher you can take that eight and flip those people and do it again. And it's unlimited for nursing homes, daycare centers, shelters, any type of emergency assistance facility. Those services have the right to basically vouch for unlimited people in their care.

Q: One of the ways we know election fraud occurs is you have large numbers of absentee ballots all being mailed to the same location.

Weible: In South Dakota we have a term called Mail 40 Locations. These are businesses where you can actually establish residency in the state so you can have your RV and travel the United States and still have a place to claim residency and file taxes and vote in elections. And so in 2018 one of these went out of business in Madison, South Dakota. When they didn't renew their business name, I paid $10 and registered that name myself. Now I'm the proud owner of this South Dakota address and the 1700 registered voters that came with it.

Q: So for my hypothetical election campaign, that's 1700 votes in the bag?

Weible: Yes.

Question: What about audits? People often say, the audits have not revealed systematic fraud, certainly not enough to tip the election.

White: If you're going to cheat, the cheat has been done beforehand. You're going to take the same ballots that have already been put in fraudulently, and recount those ballots. So you're going to get the same number every time.

Q: You're saying it's like a bank where the real money and the counterfeit money are now mixed together.

Weible: Absolutely right. And when we look at post-election audits, they're only looking at a certain percentage of precincts and a certain percentage of the races. When you do the math, it's equivalent to calling the IRS when they want to do an audit for you, handing them one day of receipts, and saying, we're good, right? It's a complete joke.

White: Yeah, because once the envelope is taken away from the ballot, you have nothing.

Q: This is a key point that I don't think most people realize. Absentee ballots only have signatures on the envelope. There is no signature on the ballot. Once the ballot and the envelope are separated, it's a permanent divorce. There is no way to go back and rejoin them.

White: Exactly. The cheat is already in.

Q: Rick, you're my consultant. It's Election Day. We're doing pretty well. We've got a lot of ballots in there, but the numbers are coming in. It's getting late in the evening. I'm nervous because I'm still behind. I need to dump another batch of ballots to put me clearly over the top. I don't want to leave this to chance. How can you help?

Weible: We have insiders that have backpacks. They are ready to go in after the polls close to start working at the vote center. And we can swap them out on site.

Q: What do you mean by that? The insider comes out with an empty backpack. You have a similar backpack and you swap the two backpacks. The guy walks back in, and now his backpack has a bunch of ballots.

Weible: We could do it that way. If we have our people as poll workers, there are many opportunities during shift changes and at other times to insert ballots where we need them.

Q: What mechanisms are in place equivalent to, say, a metal detector to make sure no one is bringing in ballots or taking them out?

Weible: Hardly any. There is too much chaos happening there on the floor.

White: I've actually observed those voter offices and watched the people just simply walk in and walk out. I've actually walked in with other people and then realized we're in the counting center. No one checks anything. No one checks our backpack. So if you have ballots in a backpack you can put them under the table.

Q: And even if later someone looks at the surveillance and goes, wait, I see a backpack full of ballots. All you've got to say . . .

White: I found them under the table, and I'm pulling them out here. Look, we found some more ballots. Who's going to question you? All you're saying is that you found the ballots.

Q: And this way even if the other guy is leading, I come through at the end and win, just like Biden and Harris did in 2020.

White: That's how the game is played. And it's going to occur at nighttime. If we're losing, the game is going to occur at nighttime.

No discussion of this topic of election fraud is possible today without taking note of the more than 10 million illegals that the Biden Harris regime has let into the country in just four years. The illegals, I'd like to suggest, are a way to make illicit additions to the voter rolls. Collectively they represent a way to create new voter rolls. And they are here in numbers quite enough to sway any presidential election. Illegals, of course, are not permitted to vote legally. If they did, they would be breaking the law. But of course illegals are confirmed lawbreakers. They broke the law to get into the country. So it's hardly astonishing to consider the prospect of them breaking the law in another fashion a second time. When lawbreakers face no penalties, they keep doing it as long as it benefits them.

Moreover, we're not really talking here about large numbers of illegals voting of their own accord. Illegals have no real motivation to engage in election fraud. On the other hand, the regime that facilitated this large-scale invasion of the country does. It simply has to engineer a system for voter registration forms to be submitted in the names of those illegals. These forms are routinely distributed to illegals when they get driver's licenses or enroll in the welfare system to get benefits. The registration forms require a single box to be checked that asks the question, "Are you a US citizen?" No proof of citizenship is required beyond this simple attestation. And is there any nationwide system in place to make sure that the answer given on those forms is verified, and the non-citizens removed from the voter rolls? There is not.[95] Consequently, once the illicit names are added to the rolls, it is simply a matter of dumping large numbers of ballots reflecting those names into the mail-in dropboxes. If anyone bothers to compare the envelopes to the voter rolls, they will see find the matching names there and wrongly conclude that these are legitimate votes.

When I interviewed Lara Trump, co-chair of the Republican National Committee, for the film, she expressed astonishment at the idea that ballots could be made and filled out and delivered, in the manner described in this chapter. She called it "horrifying." And quite clearly the RNC is going to look into it. Lara Trump assured me that election integrity is now the RNC's top priority. They are taking up the issue somewhat late in the game, but at least they are on it now. And I asked Trump himself whether he could, and would, fix the problem of election fraud once and for all if he's re-elected. You'll find his answer in the Afterword to this book.

Lincoln's solution to the breakdown of the rule of law, which he gives toward the end of his Lyceum speech, is for good citizens to mobilize against the lawbreakers, to defeat their malevolent schemes, and to recommit ourselves to the system of laws that is enshrined in the founding documents of our constitutional republic. If we don't, Lincoln knew, and we do too, then pretty soon lawbreaking of the kind we see in Venezuela and other banana republics will become institutionalized in this country and we will no longer have a constitutional republic. The American experiment will have come to a tragic end.

CHAPTER 7

THE SPIRIT OF MAGADONIA

Resistance to usurpation is possible provided the citizens understand their rights and are disposed to defend them.[96]
— Alexander Hamilton, *The Federalist Papers*

During the 1860 Republican Convention, a group of prominent East Coast Republicans met for the first time with Abraham Lincoln. They were considering him for their party's presidential nomination, but they wanted to check him out. And after a long meeting, they were largely persuaded. One elderly sage was heard to mutter, "We might have chosen a handsomer article, but I doubt whether a better."[97] This was intended humorously, but it also conveyed the Republican ambivalence over Lincoln at that time. Yes, we need him, but we wish he were better looking! Or yes he's our guy but we wish he had not given that "House Divided" speech!

In other words, the Republican establishment could only permit itself a qualified defense of Lincoln, even though, with hindsight, we see that Lincoln was precisely the man of the hour, he was perfectly suited to the crisis of 1860, and even his strange appearance—gaunt face, piercing eyes, somewhat ridiculous proportions—took on an epic grandeur as the Civil War unfolded. The wise old men of the GOP underestimated Lincoln; in retrospect, they picked not only the best man for the job but the best-looking man in the field.

In this book I have undertaken to make an unqualified defense of Trump. Not a defense that says, "I'm not sure about the guy, but I like his policies." Or, "He did a good job the last time, but I just wish he would keep his mouth shut." Or, "I have real issues with Trump, but I can't vote for what the Democrats have been doing to the country over the past four years." I have tried to show that this condescension toward Trump is entirely out of place. We don't need to revise or fix Trump. We don't need to rehabilitate him. Trump doesn't need to do this or that to deserve our support. He doesn't need to change. First of all, he's not going to change—this should be obvious to anyone even remotely familiar with him—but the more important point is that he doesn't need to. He ain't broke; so don't try to fix him.

We're the ones that are broke; we need to fix ourselves. Trump doesn't need a rehabilitation scheme; we do. We are, for the most part, impoverished in our understanding of Trump, in our lack of appreciation for him as a man and as a leader. We need to get our clocks fixed and recognize what time it is in this country. We also need to look inwardly and compare our own personality and character to Trump's, to see how we really stack up. When I compare Trump's moral character to virtually anyone else in the political sphere, I find that he is far superior in this decisive respect.

The reason we miss this—and by we, I'm referring to traditional Republicans, not to the MAGA loyalists—is because we have been conned by the Left and the media to focus on Trump's vices, while ignoring his great strengths. Sure, Trump has vices as we all do, and as the very people who impugn him do. "He's a liar." No, he's an exaggerator, as all salesman are. "He's mean." And how would you respond if you were subjected to the lies, hatred, and fury that he gets every day? "He's a playboy." Again, are you sure you would resist that temptation if you were in his position in his younger days?

Trump is obviously not a playboy now, so the worst we can say about him is that he is a reformed playboy. "He's egotistical." True, but I repeat what I said earlier: this vice—and it is a vice—has become in today's circumstances a political virtue. Why? Because Trump's ego insulates him from the abuse and the criminal charges and the unceasing parade of horrors that would surely have crushed a more modest man, like the main character Joseph K. in Kafka's *The Trial*, who eventually crumbles and starts to believe the lies about himself.

We hear, even from Republicans, about Trump's vices, but what about his virtues? He's an optimistic, forward-looking guy. He's affable, even in circumstances when most people would not be. He's a terrific parent and grandparent, as evidenced by how his family has turned out and how close they are to him. He's patriotic, and makes sacrifices and takes risks to do what he does because he loves his country. He's generous, and big-hearted, which can be confirmed not by his contributions to the opera house or the visible charities, but rather by the way he treats the people who work for him. He's not pompous or elitist in his manner; he identifies with the lives and concerns of ordinary people. Quite obviously, he cares about them. He's loyal, and values loyalty in others; the quality he hates most in people is betrayal and treachery, and that according to Dante is the worst of the human qualities, which is why Dante puts the traitors and betrayers alongside Satan in the lowest circle of hell.[98] Finally, Trump is brave, but he's not just brave in the ordinary sense; his bravery is surpassing, sui generis, almost superhuman. If you doubt this, ask yourself who could endure what Trump has, from character assassination to legal assassination to attempted assassination, and push forward with such insouciance and aplomb.

So far throughout this book, I've been developing an elaborate interpretation of Trump through the lens of Lincoln and his Lyceum speech. There is another way, also using a late nineteenth-century analogy, to understand Trump. Before I came to America, I had no direct familiarity with Americans or American culture. My knowledge was largely through the lens of movies, most commonly Westerns. I saw a whole bunch of them, and my favorites include *For a Few Dollars More* starring Clint Eastwood and *The Man Who Shot Liberty Valance* starring Jimmy Stewart and John Wayne. The Western is, above all, a morality tale and, as such, it provides a remarkably clear and insightful way to look at Donald Trump and our current crisis.

In the typical Western, we first see a small town, which is generally named Shinbone or Pleasantville or something like that. A quiet place, with happy people, and an old sheriff with a toothbrush mustache. The sheriff is a good guy, but he is a man of platitudes. He disdains the excessive use of force; he envisions a kinder, gentler Shinbone. And in a peaceful environment, his approach is the right one. People gather for drinks and conviviality at the local saloon. They get their foodstuffs at the local provision store.

Then the harmony of the town is viciously disrupted when the gangsters arrive. The arrival of the gangsters is highlighted with a shocking display of murderous depravity. This is intended to convey to the audience that the old harmony is gone. Shinbone is not the same place that it was before the gangsters arrived. With ruthless dispatch, the outlaws take over the town. They take over the saloon and the provision store. They overpower the old sheriff and, in doing so, the outlaws become the law. They insult the young girls and women. They terrify the population into submission. Shinbone now faces an existential threat. The evil is consolidating itself; it seems invincible.

And then, over the mountain, comes a lone rider. He's an outsider; not a lot is known about him. The townspeople aren't sure what to make of him, because he's rough, he seems uncouth, and most of all they don't know what his motives are. But the gangsters recognize right away that this man is their real threat. He is normal on the surface, but he is also, as the bad guys immediately realize, a figure of uncommon strength and power. And he has their number. The gangsters put him to the test, and he quickly shows that despite his evident circumspection, he has no intention of submitting to their authority. So they resolve to destroy him in one way or another. They will stop at nothing. They try to buy him off, to intimidate him, to turn the people of the town against him, even to beat him up and kill him.

But the man proves uncommonly resilient. He takes some heavy blows, but he doesn't go down for good. He is persistent. He is strategic. And he's very quick on the draw. He is a match—more than a match—for the bad guys put together. And eventually there is the great shootout or the great draw. The gangsters have rigged the odds. Despite their superiority in firepower, they are determined to cheat. The hero is onto the cheating, but he is not himself a cheater. He fights fair and shoots straight. And in the end, through sheer mastery of the arts of combat, he defeats the gangsters. Sometimes this is accomplished with the help of some allies from the town; sometimes he does this all by himself. Either way, the bad guys get their comeuppance.

But then we get to the crucial ending scene, and it is typically the same. The threat from the gangsters is over. Not permanently— because new gangsters can always show up. But it is over, for now. And the townspeople are jubilant and grateful. Some of them would like the outsider to stay. He might be needed to deal with new gangsters in the future. But the man never stays. He gets on his horse and he rides away. Now why does he do this? The reason is a subtle, but important one. The outsider could have stayed. In fact, he could have ruled the town as a gangster himself. He has shown he has the power to defeat the gangsters, so he could easily become the new gangster. But our hero doesn't want to do this, and this is what makes him our hero. His goal is to make Shinbone great again. And having done his job, he leaves. And in doing so, he shows the town that he was always on their side. Before that, the people knew he was against the gangsters, but they didn't know he was for them. In the end, they know.

That's fiction, the way we like it. But it is also reality in America today. I shared my analogy with Lara Trump and she loved it. "We are living," she responded, "in an actual American Western right now." Incredibly, the fictional has become real. This is the story of Donald Trump. But now we have a conundrum, and just as we opened this book with a conundrum, we close it with one. If Trump is the hero of the American story, why doesn't everyone on his own side recognize it? We can understand why the Democrats despise him; he stands to ruin their wicked and tyrannical schemes. But what about the Republican Party?

I'm not talking about the MAGA Republicans, or even the rank and file Republicans who mostly now "get" Trump. I'm talking about the Republican establishment, represented in the Westerns by the sheriff and the old guard of the town. The Republican establishment recognizes the alarming way in which surveillance, ideological propaganda, censorship, and criminalization of political differences have all crept into our society in just a few short years. They are aware that we are living in a country far removed from the constitutional republic our founders devised; indeed, that we are governed by a regime that calls itself "progressive," by which they mean progress away from the American founding. In a sense, the country itself is facing an assassination attempt.

Like the old guard in the movies, the GOP establishment is aware of the nature of the threat. They've seen what Obama did to the country, and then Biden and Harris, and they understand that Harris and Walz will take things even further. So they know the danger is real. But in the movies, even the old guard has no difficulty recognizing the significance of the arrival of Clint Eastwood or John Wayne. They know they themselves are not up to the job of taking on the gangsters. They see he's their best, indeed their only hope. They don't say, "This guy is so flawed." "Our problem with him is that he's not a family man." "Tell him to stop waving his gun around so much. It's polarizing." They don't form groups that call themselves #NeverWayne or #NeverEastwood. On the contrary, they recognize that, in their dire circumstances, the outsider is the only one that can save them.

So what's with the GOP? I'm going to answer this question, but I'd like to do it in a roundabout way, by posing another—related—question. I'll answer this other question, and then *en passant* I'll provide the answer to this one. Two answers for the price of one! Here then is my second or other question: What gives the Left and the Democrats the chutzpah to do what they are doing? What makes them think they can get away with squelching our free speech, restricting our freedom of assembly, charging us with bogus crimes, mobilizing the weaponry of the Justice Department against us, seeking to lock up our party nominee, and in general running roughshod over our basic constitutional rights and terrorizing us in the manner of a police state?

My answer to this question can be given in the line that Cassius says regarding Caesar.

He would not be a wolf
But that he sees the Romans are but sheep.[99]

In other words, Caesar becomes so tyrannical only because he knows

that the Romans are willing to be subjected to tyranny. And here's how
this point applies to our situation. We're all familiar with the phrase,
"Critical Race Theory." Let's ignore the race part and focus just on the
word critical. It means analytical. It refers to the first thing you do,
which is to carefully observe and study your adversary. This is what the
Left and the Democrats have been doing. They have been studying us.
And what have they concluded? That we—the patriots and conservatives and Republicans and Christians—are in general the party of the
namby-pambies. From their point of view—and truth be told, from
ours also—we are the party of live and let live, of civility and good
manners, of giving our opponents the benefit of the doubt, of rising
above their underhanded tactics and refusing to follow suit, of standing
on high principle, of turning the other cheek. In short, we are precisely
the invertebrate wimps that the other side was hoping for. The party
of pusillanimity.

Our pusillanimity encourages their aggression. They say to themselves, why don't we go ahead and try to stack the Supreme Court?
It doesn't matter if we fail, because we know the other side is too
"principled" to do the same. They are congenitally wedded to having nine justices on the Court. So even if we fail, we'll come back
and try again. And in a similar vein, why don't we censor and stig-
matize and ostracize them? They don't have the power to do the
same to us, and even if they did, they wouldn't do it. Come to think
of it, let's also deploy the institutions of the state—the FBI, CIA,
the NSA, the IRS, the DOJ, DHS, even the military—against them.
Again, they would never dream of doing the same to us, even if
they were in power and in a position to do so. They wouldn't lower
themselves to our standards—at least that's how those idiots see it—
which means that we can continue to torment them with impunity.
Who wouldn't want to take on such losers?

The Left and the Democrats are in the position of the schoolyard bully who has complete sway over his terrified victims. And the GOP establishment are the terrified ones. They are terrified of the Democrats. They are terrified of the media. They are terrified of being called "election deniers" and "insurrectionists." Mitch McConnell and Mike Johnson live in fear that if the media were to target them and mercilessly assail them, they would be so badly wounded that their own side would bury them. Consequently the GOP establishment operates as if its only viable strategy is to appease the bully, even though they know, deep down, that bullies can never be appeased, and any appeasement is only short lived, and in the end the bully gets so strong that he doesn't even need their appeasement. That's when he throws them all into the ditch, enjoying himself immensely as he does it. Tyranny, let's not forget, is immensely enjoyable to tyrants.

But here comes Trump, who is himself—in his own way—a bully. Trump doesn't bully people who are below him, but he is quite capable of bullying other bullies. He even seems to enjoy it, in his own way. He likes seeing bullies get their comeuppance. In a certain way, he has qualities that resemble those of his adversaries. In Shakespeare's *Coriolanus*, we see that Coriolanus is a warrior and Aufidius is a warrior and even though they are on opposite sides, there is a kind of kinship between them.[100] So the Democrats recognize Trump as their foil. This is easy to understand.

But why don't the establishment Republicans, and even some rank and file Republicans, see that Trump is both willing and able to do it? Why don't they get behind him if he is ready to lead the fight? The puzzle is deepened when we see that these people are not capable of taking on the Democrats themselves—and they know it. Former President George W. Bush said in 2016, "I'm worried that I will be the last Republican president."[101] What an admission! Bush basically concedes that his GOP—the GOP as it evolved over twenty-five years, from his father to him—is basically a lost cause. Why, then, would this band of losers refuse to rally behind a new leader who can win?

I believe the answer is that not only are many of these people cowards, but they have figured out a way to turn cowardliness itself into a virtue. In other words, to their great sin of cowardice they have added the sin of self-delusion. They are cowards who think they are models of character and rectitude. Let's turn to the philosopher Nietzsche for some insight on this. Nietzsche writes in *Thus Spoke Zarathustra*, "So much kindness, so much weakness do I see. Round, fair and considerate are they to one another, as grains of sand are round, fair and considerate to grains of sand. At bottom, they want a single thing most of all: that no one hurt them. Thus they try to please and gratify everybody. That, however, is cowardice, even if it be called virtue. But they lack fists: their fingers do not know how to creep behind fists. Virtue for them is that which makes modest and tame: with that they have turned the wolf into a dog, and man himself into man's best domestic animal."[102]

Nietzsche's aphoristic style takes some getting used to, but what is he saying here? He's saying that cowards don't like to admit to themselves that they are cowardly. They don't want to look in the mirror. And so they figure out a way to convert their cowardice into virtue, their weakness into an imaginary form of strength. They say that they refuse to fight because they are too good to fight. They are too noble to lower themselves to take on the bully. They are better than the bully, and the bully's tactics are morally objectionable to them. Even if the bully smashes them in the face, they will not gang up on the bully and kick him in the shins. They will not teach the bully the only kind of lesson that would convince the bully to stop being a bully.

And since they know that Trump is willing to deal with the bully in the only manner that bullies recognize, they deplore Trump and accuse him of being the worst kind of bully himself. They ask, "Why can't you fight those bullies without using bullying tactics yourselves? Why can't you fight virtuously like we do?" This of course is not intended as a serious argument; rather, as Nietzsche points out, it is a salve for their sick consciences. These weak and pathetic creatures can only live with themselves by convincing themselves that their groveling nature is indeed the greatest moral virtue of all. They are in the mode of the craven deserter who tells himself that true courage is running away from the battlefield.

So what is the story that these GOP establishment types tell themselves? They tell themselves that things used to be better in the Reagan and Bush era. It was, in George H. W. Bush's own words, a "kinder, gentler America." I am a product of that era myself, and served in my twenties as a policy analyst in the Reagan White House. I also worked on George H. W. Bush's 1992 presidential campaign. To a degree, nostalgia for that era is understandable. It was a time when I lived in Washington, DC and had many liberal friends. I was especially close to some of the people who are now Never Trump; they were my colleagues at the American Enterprise Institute. But it is the beginning of political wisdom to recognize that we are no longer living in the Reagan Bush era. It would be like a pioneer family whose homestead is surrounded by outlaws saying to each other, "Let's all wish that Shinbone was the way it was before the outlaws showed up."

Of course there will be some in the GOP camp—notably the Never Trump people—who will say that Trump is the cause of the division and polarization that has occurred subsequent to the Reagan era. But this is manifestly untrue. Trump didn't cause the division; it would be more accurate to say that it caused him. The division was started, at least embryonically, in the Clinton years, not so much by Bill as by Hillary. Then Obama introduced political targeting by corrupting and unleashing the IRS and the police agencies of government against Republicans and conservatives. Trump came on the scene to question, challenge and expose the corruption and the emerging tyranny, and he did. But it got worse—far worse—over the past four years under Biden and Harris.

Yes, but didn't Trump break with the ideological orthodoxy of Reaganism? There are several things to be said here. First, the general principles of Reaganism were peace through strength in foreign policy, free markets, and the aspiration of upward mobility in domestic policy, and traditional values including pro-life and an affirmation of family values in social policy. These are still the guiding principles of Trump and the MAGA movement. True, Trump doesn't like getting us in foreign wars through the deployment of US troops, but Reagan didn't either. Reagan didn't even send troops when the Soviet Union invaded Afghanistan with 100,000 soldiers. Nor did Reagan launch any preemptive attacks on any other country.

We forget that Reagan's policies in foreign, domestic, and social policy were for the most part pragmatic and transactional. Reagan was pugnaciously anti-Soviet during his first term, and then he turned around and affably did business with the new Soviet leader Gorbachev in his second. Trump is transactional in very much the same way. In theory, he's against getting into foreign entanglements, but he's quite willing to order lethal strikes on al-Baghdadi and Soleimani. He is not above threatening the Chinese or the Russians that if they cross the line, he will bomb Beijing or Moscow. In domestic policy Trump cut taxes just like Reagan did, although not as much as Reagan did, and in social policy Trump, through his Supreme Court appointments, brought about the downfall of *Roe v. Wade*, which Reagan was not able to do. Ironically, it was Trump, and not Reagan or Bush, who proved to be the most pro-life president the Republicans have ever had.

The MAGA movement, it is true, has a different thrust and a different feel than Reaganism. I want to argue that this is not because its principles are alien to Reaganism, but rather because the America we live in now is alien to the America of the 1980s and 1990s. Reagan's America is now the world we have lost, and the best way to get it back is not to foolishly pine for bygone days, but to resolutely apply Reaganite principles to the new and far more grim situation in which we find ourselves. This, the GOP establishment is reluctant to do; this the Never Trump movement refuses to do. One group maunders incoherently in the manner of the trusty old sheriff who has lost all his power but still pretends to be in charge; the other has slyly thrown its lot in with the gangsters and stridently insists that the outsider, not the gangsters, represent the real threat to law and order in Shinbone.

Consider the inane pyrotechnics of the leading anti-Trump and Never Trump figures in the GOP. Nikki Haley and Bill Barr say they'll vote for Trump because the Democrats are worse; this is like expressing reluctant support for John Wayne because he's presumed to be a bad guy but not as bad as the gangsters and outlaws who have taken over the town. Mike Pence, Chris Christie, and Paul Ryan say that Trump is unfit for office but they are not going to vote for the Democrats. Imagine a scene in *The Man Who Shot Liberty Valance* in which some influential townsmen refuse to choose between the hero, played by John Wayne, and the outlaw Liberty Valance and his bloodthirsty gang. And then there are the Never Trump operatives—Bill Kristol, Adam Kinzinger, Joe Walsh—who have endorsed Harris and, in effect, signed up to serve with the Valance outlaws, all while holding themselves up as protectors of the town and of the high principles of democracy, public accountability, and law and order.

There is, regrettably, a Christian counterpart to this madness. Here I'll make the point not in reference to Western films but an episode right out of the Bible. We read in the Old Testament of the rise of the young warrior David and the desperate battle between the Israelites and the Philistines. The Philistines are the radical secularists of their day; in fact, they are pagans. They utterly reject the monotheistic God of the Israelites. They join the Canaanites and the Hittites in worshipping Baal and they also engage in depraved and bloodthirsty sexual practices. In short, they are the ancient incarnation of today's Democratic Party.

One would think that, in this situation, the Israelites would unify behind David. He is the bravest of the group, and he has the power to defeat the Philistines. He has proven this by toppling the Philistine giant Goliath, much in the same way that Trump proved his mettle by dispatching Hillary Clinton. But now imagine if a group of Israelites insisted that, for them to get behind David, he would have to meet their standards. "David must change. He must stop carrying around that slingshot. He needs to be more like us." The problem with this, of course, is that if David were more like them, he would be in their same miserable situation regarding the Philistines. And then imagine, on top of this, an indignant Never David camp that insists it would be immoral to join with David because of that Bathsheba business. "David has proven that he doesn't have the character to lead us in this battle. We need to find someone else." It is bad enough to spout such twisted nonsense under normal circumstances, but to do it when the fate of the society itself is at stake is the height of reckless immorality. As we see from my Old Testament example, God did not hesitate to choose

David, which means that God did not hold Himself to such peculiar and absurd standards!

Aristotle writes somewhere that "natural right is changeable." I first encountered this enigmatic Aristotelian dictum in the writings of the philosopher Leo Strauss.[103] And I have pondered this claim for more than twenty years. At first glance it seems highly problematic and strange. How can the very principles of right and wrong—what the ancient Greeks called natural right—be changeable? Wouldn't this be akin to saying the Ten Commandments is changeable? I think the best way to understand Aristotle here is that while the principles remain the same, the application changes depending on the circumstances. And this seems the best way to understand the MAGA movement. It is an intelligent and necessary response to the deterioration of the country since the Reagan era. It is a new application of old principles in a way that might actually work. Clearly, the old principles applied in the old way are inadequate to the current situation.

Consider a simple example of this, which applies to Trump and also to my own work. In my 1995 book *The End of Racism*, I showed how Blacks fall behind other groups on all measures of academic achievement and economic performance. I argued that such inferiority was not due to racism and it was not due to genes; rather, it was due to cultural habits and cultural backwardness.[104] In taking this approach, I was squarely within the conservative understanding of race going back to Bill Buckley and the early days of *National Review*. I was pursuing what might be termed a "racism minimization" strategy. Basically, this approach says that racism is not such a big deal, at least not anymore, and that Black whining about racism is out of place. In its extreme form, this approach even involves diminishing the horrors of slavery and segregation.

But if you watch my film *Hillary's America*, which was released in 2016, you'll see an entirely different approach. Far from being downplayed, slavery and racism are highlighted in that film. The true horrors of both are dramatically emphasized. There are scenes of slave whippings, and of Blacks being terrorized by the night riders of the Ku Klux Klan. No racial minimization strategy here! Instead, the emphasis is entirely different. The film exposes the full extent to which slavery, segregation, racial terrorism, Jim Crow—the whole shop of horrors—was perpetrated by the Democratic Party. Yes, these things were just as horrific as the Blacks tell us, but we didn't do it, the Democrats did.

Now, in theory both approaches are rooted in facts and truth. The country has indeed come a long way since the bad old days of the past. Buckley and his cohorts at *National Review* were right about that. But in embracing the racial minimization strategy they often made common cause with the Confederacy and with the Democratic bigots of the twentieth-century South. Consequently, they drove Blacks away from the Republican Party, or, more precisely, since Blacks had already moved over to the Democratic camp by that time, they reinforced Black allegiance to the Democrats— the very party that had unleashed the worst barbarism in American history on them. The approach of *Hillary's America*, by contrast, was to invite Blacks to return to the Republican Party—the party of Lincoln. By emphasizing the historical atrocities of the Democrats, the movie opened the eyes of many Blacks to a whole narrative that has been assiduously suppressed in progressive textbooks and in the progressive media. The Left, after all, is not eager to inform Blacks about how the Democrats enslaved, whipped, tortured, and burned them.

Consequently, *Hillary's America* and my subsequent films have done more to draw Blacks into the Republican camp than all my earlier work on affirmative action and *The End of Racism*. To pick up Aristotle's dictum, my principles haven't changed but my application has. This shift in my own work corresponds to the way in which MAGA and now the mainstream of the Republican Party have shifted from one approach to another. The shift is also reflected in Trump's own approach. You'll never hear Trump talk about how racism might once have been a problem but now it's no big deal. On the contrary, Trump emphasizes how Democratic policies keep Blacks on a new type of plantation, and how Republican policies offer a way out for groups long trapped in poverty and dependency by Democrats who couldn't care less about Black welfare. Trump, in other words, stresses the continuity of American history—the Democrats are taking advantage of Blacks now, just as they have before.

This shift in the way that Trump and we MAGA Republicans approach the race issue has been critical in creating the possibility of the GOP becoming the party of the working class—not just the white working class but also the Black working class and the Latino working class. The prospect of Black and Latino blue-collar workers coming over to Trump is not merely a political nightmare; it is virtually impossible for Democrats and the Left to come to terms with intellectually. The only way they can do so is to accuse the defecting Blacks and Latinos of being wannabe white supremacists. Geraldo Cadava's article, "The Rise of Latino White Supremacy" published in the *New Yorker*, is a classic of the genre, as is a recent NPR discussion, "Understanding Multiracial Whiteness and Trump Supporters."[105]

Progressive bellyaching is not going to stop the trend. Now, as never before, the GOP actually has the chance to win over the entire FDR coalition. FDR helped to make the Democrats the party of the white, Black and Hispanic working class. The GOP has an historic opportunity to win these voters now, and if it does it could be the majority party for the next generation. It couldn't do it, however, by continuing its old mantra of notifying minority voters that reports of the incidence of racism, both in the past and now, are highly exaggerated.

Let me turn now to a more controversial application of the Aristotelian dictum. Trump has suggested, on more than one occasion, that if elected once again he will retaliate against the Democrats and the police agencies of the government for what they have attempted to do to him and to his allies. And this is a theme that has been taken up in at least some quarters of the MAGA movement. Attorney Mike Davis, for instance, has suggested statutes under which leading Democratic officials could be prosecuted for attempting to violate the constitutional liberties of their fellow Americans. [106]

One promising example is 18 U.S.C. 241, which makes it a felony for "two or more persons to agree to injure, threaten or intimidate a person in the United States in the free exercise or enjoyment of ay right or privilege secured by the Constitution or laws of the United States or because of his or her having exercised such a right." And 18 U.S.C. 242 makes it a crime for someone in government, acting "under color of law," to "willfully deprive a person of a right or privilege protected by the Constitution or laws of the United States." [107] I can think of dozens of prosecutions of leading Democrats, both inside and outside the government, that can be brought under these two provisions alone. Not surprisingly, Democrats like Chuck Schumer and Gretchen Whitmer shriek that Trump is threatening to go after his political opponents! Coming from them, this accusation carries no credibility or weight, because this is precisely what they have been doing for the past several years.

But what about concerns, expressed by some Republicans, that

Trump is simply after "vengeance" and that this is all about him? First of all, it's worth pointing out that in the old Westerns, vengeance is never a bad motive. Vengeance is always justified! The bad guys are so evil that it is simply unacceptable for the hero to do anything less than to finish them off. It simply wouldn't do to give them a beating and send them skulking out of town. And if this seems like an antique code from the nineteenth century, consider that it met the approval of movie audiences in the middle of the twentieth century, so it's not so antique after all.

Is Trump expected, in the face of what he has endured, to simply turn the other cheek? It's worth remembering that Jesus didn't always turn the other cheek himself. Consider the encounter with the high priests when Jesus is struck by one of the guards following his arrest in the Garden of Gethsemane. Jesus doesn't say, "That was a nice blow. Now give me another." Rather, he says, "Why do you strike me?" And then there is Jesus overturning the tables of the moneychangers in the temple, driving them out of the premises without mercy or hesitation. Christians who have reservations about Trump might do well to reflect on the biblical injunction in Matthew 10:16, "Behold, I am sending you out as sheep in the midst of wolves, so be wise as serpents and innocent as doves." The reference to serpents is odd, because the serpent in Scripture is associated with evil. But Matthew also associates the serpent with wisdom: the wisdom to camouflage itself when it is targeted by predators, and also the wisdom to strike suddenly and venomously at the enemy.

The moral question before us—one that MAGA has already supplied its answer to—is whether this serpentine wisdom has a current-day application. Specifically, is it right for us to do to them what they have been doing to us? Admittedly this question was unimaginable during the Reagan era. Reagan or George H. W. Bush would never dream, for example, of putting filmmaker Michael Moore in jail. But then neither would Jimmy Carter have dreamed of putting a conservative filmmaker like me in jail. In other words, we didn't have to consider this solution in Reagan's time because the problem did not exist.

But interestingly enough, it existed in Lincoln's time. Early in the Civil War, the Union Army for the first time deployed Black troops. There weren't that many of them. The Civil War was, for the most part, a white man's fight. But even so, there were some Black soldiers, and if you've seen the movie *Glory*, it memorializes their valor. The Confederates were so outraged at the prospect of having to fight against Blacks, however, that their leader Jefferson Davis issued an edict saying that any Black union soldier captured by the Confederacy would be shot. This did not apply to white union soldiers, who would become normal prisoners of war. But for Black captives, it would be a different fate. Abraham Lincoln learned of this edict, and in 1863—in a scene captured in one of my films, where Lincoln is on a train and enveloped in smoke—he signed what historians call the Order of Retaliation. Basically it says that for any Black union soldier captured and killed by the Confederacy, one Confederate captive will be executed.[108]

Now why would Lincoln, a moderate man, issue an order of such barbarity? Why would he do something that would today be condemned under the Geneva Convention and the laws of war? The reason is obvious. Lincoln realized that he had to do to them what they had been doing to him, otherwise they would never stop. Remarkably, the Confederates, upon learning of Lincoln's order, did stop, and Lincoln then promptly withdrew the order.

The lesson is that it's not about vengeance; it's about how to stop the tyrannical abuses of the Left. Clearly writing a strongly-worded op-ed is not going to do the trick. Bullies and outlaws understand a single language, the language of force. This is not to suggest that

Trump or the MAGA movement is calling for lawlessness. On the contrary, they are calling for holding the outlaws accountable to the full force of the law. They want to put the outlaws behind bars, both to discourage them from relying in future on outlaw ways, and also to deter other potential outlaws. And there is nothing immoral about this. Deploying force on behalf of law is not the moral equivalent of deploying the forces of lawlessness. If it were, then the cops on the street would be the moral equivalent of the criminals.

Can Trump win? The Democrats know he can! Already they are mobilizing against what they consider to be the terrifying prospect of a second Trump term.[109] But Trump's victory in 2024 is not inevitable. We must mobilize all our forces to make it happen. And in every way, from how we win the election to how we govern the country, we should be ready for them, as they are getting ready for us. Trump and MAGA are nothing less than a survival plan for America. There is no other survival plan. We can either stand by and watch the nation destroyed by the forces of evil and tyranny, or we can rally behind Trump and the MAGA movement and begin the process—and it will be a long and laborious process—of restoring the country and making America great again.

AN EXCLUSIVE INTERVIEW WITH DONALD TRUMP

This conversation took place at Mar-a-Lago on July 23, 2024. It has been slightly edited for clarity.

Question: President Trump, here we are in Mar-a-Lago. It is magnificent. It's a castle. And every room more beautiful than the next. And I look at the White House and I think that's like low-income housing. That's nothing compared to this place right here. So my first question to you is, why do you do it?

Former President Donald J. Trump: To be honest, I do it because I love our country and this country has tremendous potential. It's been horribly run over a fairly long period of time, and it's been hurt badly. It's a failing nation in many respects. I think you understand that better than most. People took over and they destroyed our country. They really did. They allowed millions of people to come into our country from prisons and from mental institutions and terrorists. And look at all of the problems that we have now. It's so sad to see. So I felt I had no right not to do it. I thought I had almost an obligation to do it.

Q: What do you love most about America?

Trump: I just love the concept of freedom. I see other countries, I know other countries, I know the heads of other countries, and I see how they do things. But we're getting there a little bit right now as of this date. We're getting there. We're fascist. You could call it whatever you want. You know very well yourself what they've done to you. It's a persecution. And it's become a nastier place, a much nastier place. And we're going to turn that around.

Q: Before I came to America, I was exposed to movies, Western movies, and here's the plot of the typical Western: You have a small town. It's running pretty well. You got some old sheriff with a toothbrush mustache, and he's, you know, he's doing just fine. But then some really bad guys come in, some outlaws, they take over the town, they take over the institutions, they take over the saloon, they beat up the old sheriff. They're running the place. And then an outsider comes in over the mountain. It's Clint Eastwood, it's John Wayne, and right away the bad guys realize this is the threat. This is the guy we gotta watch out for. We got to go after this guy and take him out because he poses a threat to us. And I say to myself, that's you. I mean, we're living, in a sense, in the plot of a Western. What do you think?

Trump: So many people come up to me and they say, you are our last hope. You are our last hope. And they mean it. It's very sophisticated people, incredibly, incredibly sophisticated people. They really see what's happening with our country. And, they say we're becoming like Venezuela. They say all sorts of things. You know that happens quickly. You go back twenty years ago, Venezuela was a much different place. You go back twenty years ago, a lot of places were a lot different. And usually when they go bad, it's very, very hard to come back. And it would be the same for this country. You know, there are those that say this will be our last election. If we don't win, this could be our last election. And I fully understand what they mean. It's a very dangerous time for our country.

Q: And would you agree that we're dealing not just with incompetence, but we're dealing with the sort of gangsterization of American politics?

Trump: Yeah, we are, we're doing that. And we have people that—I guess they're just bad people. And you don't know why. Why would they? Why would they want to have open borders with the world pouring into our country and destroying your Social Security and Medicare and taking your hospital beds and taking over your school rooms and taking everything else? And it's no good for anybody. They die coming up in the caravans. They end up doing very badly. Women are just being absolutely battered with what's going on. And why would they want men playing in women's sports? Everything wants to go woke, and woke is unhappy. You know, if you ever look at it, did you ever meet a woke person that's happy? There's no such thing. So, we've got a fight, and we're going to do well. We're going to turn it around, and I think we can do it relatively quickly.

Q: The Left and the Democrats say you want to come in a second time and you will never leave. Now you have trolled those people by putting out funny memes about Trump 24, Trump 28, Trump 32. But I think of the Western where the good guy comes in, he takes care of the bad guys, he fixes the place, and then at the end of the movie, he leaves. Can you speak to the fact that you want to fix the country and then come back to Mar-a-Lago?

Trump: Well, you know, yeah, it's very interesting. And I've seen that. I've seen it with us. "He's never going to leave if he comes back." And they said that the first time, too. "He's never going to leave." Of course I'm going to leave. And we'll have plenty of time to fix the country. And we have great people, you know, we have great back up and somebody will take over and they'll do a good job, but we want to let that person be elected fairly. They have such bad policies. They have policies that are guaranteed to fail. These policies that they have now have never worked. And they're not going to work now. So we're going to fix it, and we're going to make it, maybe better than ever.

Q: A young Abraham Lincoln in his twenties gave a famous speech called the Lyceum Speech, and in it, very early he prophesied that there might come a time in America when a dictator—he mentions Napoleon, he mentions Caesar, he mentions Alexander—would take over the country and subvert the Constitution. Now the Democrats go, yeah, of course that's Trump. He's the dictator. But I think to myself, you were in office and what did you do that was dictatorial? Nothing.

Trump: No, we were all about democracy, and that's what we're about. And, you know, the theme is, oh, Trump will subvert democracy, but they're the ones that are going to subvert democracy. And that's what they're doing all the time.

Q: I mean, did you censor anyone? No. Did you lock up any leading Democrats? No. There were people chanting for Hillary to be locked up, but you didn't lock her up.

Trump: They were doing things that were just unbelievable. With Hillary as an example, I thought it would be a terrible thing, actually. Everybody talked about it. What she did was terrible. What Biden did was terrible. What they all did. But I never would even think of doing that. But now, do we change our thinking because they've done it? What they've done with me is incredible. We just beat one of the cases in Florida, the big one, the classified documents case, and that sent them reeling. And they are crazed right now. They're absolutely crazed. But when you think of it, I could have done it. And we had them dead to rights. But wouldn't it be a terrible thing? And yet now what they've done is opened up Pandora's box. That is a very dangerous thing. They've created a very dangerous precedent.

Q: Let me tell you what I think they're doing and why they're doing it to you. It's because you're not a normal Republican. You are a massive entrepreneurial success and a builder. You built the New York skyline. You're also a cultural icon. So they fear that even though they know you're not Caesar, you do have that kind of dimension. You have that kind of power. And you didn't do an insurrection, but guess what? Had you called for one that would have been one and there would be one if you called for one now. And they know you have that kind of power and they're scared of it. And so, they're like, this is the one guy we need to go after by all means necessary.

Trump: It's wonderful of you to say that, but I'm not sure that I have that power. I'm not sure I want that power. I want the power just to make the country better. We need power to make the country better. We're way behind. When you look at the things that we have to do to catch up with other countries, you know, China is lapping us in so many different ways. And militarily especially, they're building ships at a rate ten times greater than ours. And at some point we're going to have to catch them. And if we don't catch them, there could be problems. And we have enemies in two places—inside and outside. And I think the outside ones are far less dangerous in many ways than the inside ones. We have people in the country that are truly, I don't even know if they think of themselves as enemies, but they're probably somewhat sick and they're really hurting our country, and we have to beat them. We have to beat them because there's no reasoning with them. I don't see any reasoning with them, and nobody has for a long time. So we're going to beat them. We're going to win the election. And after we win the election, we're going to straighten out our country.

Q: I mean, this is a key point, because although people talk about unity, it seems to me it's hard to unite with people who are trying to destroy America, who have an agenda that would take the country down, from which we could hardly recover. So is it your idea to unify the country against the people who want to destroy America?
Trump: Well, you know, they talk about unity, but there's such a difference. For instance, they want open borders. We want closed borders. We want people to come in legally. We want people that will help our country, not people that we're going to be taking care of, or that were in jails and we're going to now just put them in our jails, because that's what's happening. They're emptying out their jails into our country. Now, who can want that? But that's what they want. They want things that we can't give. Third world countries have borders. Nobody has a border where twenty million people come through totally unvetted and unchecked. A beautiful United States of America is receiving prisoners from all over the world. They're coming in from the Congo and Africa. They're coming in from, Yemen. They're coming in from everywhere. And the prison populations are down. You know, Venezuela, crime is way down because they've taken their criminals and they've dropped them into the United States. And if I were running those countries, I'd be doing the same thing. So can there be unity? I'm not sure. The one thing I will say is we had the most successful country we've ever had and there was unity. Believe it or not, people were getting on board. It was an amazing thing. It was happening during the period of time that I was president. There was the semblance of unity happening. I waw it happening. So I think success can bring unity.

Q: When you and I were a lot younger, we thought of America as the free world. And then over there you got the unfree world, the Soviet Union and Cuba and China and so on. But now I look at the signature defining elements of these unfree societies. Take North Korea, they have, you know, they have censorship, they have mass surveillance, they have ideological indoctrination.

Trump: We have that.

Q: I was going to say, we have criminalization of political differences. They try to lock up their leading opponent, namely you. And, so I say to myself, who's doing this? You're not doing it. You're not the dictator, but the elements of tyranny we're seeing from the Democrats, aren't they the ones doing it? Aren't they the Caesar that Lincoln warned about?

Trump: Look, if I weren't running for office and doing well, I wouldn't have any of these court cases. None of them. I have court cases all over the place, and I'm doing well. I have good lawyers. I've been doing a good job. Of course, it costs a lot of money, a lot of money. But this is the criminalization of the justice system. This is the weaponization of justice. And nobody thought it could happen in this country. Well, it has happened in this country. And it is a double pronged game. I mean, they have to be careful too, because they're setting a very bad and a very dangerous precedent. But we have, we have a justice system that speaks to local DAs—that deals with the local attorney generals. "Get Trump," they say, "Get Trump." And then the Democrats say, "We're running against a criminal." It's such a nice sound. But a lot of people don't understand that all of this stuff is done by Biden and Harris. You know, this whole thing with Biden was a fake deal. Everybody knew he was not going to make it. And I think the debate was the thing that finally showed it.

Q: It showed what a knockout artist you are. Because I mean, when before in American history has a presidential debate put the other guy out of the race?

Trump: Well, there's never been anything quite like it, actually, and that's what put him out of the race. So now what? You would think you'd want somebody very capable. We need very smart people at the head of our country. We didn't have that with Biden. And we don't have that with my current opponent, I guess.

Q: You mean the woman who informs us that we didn't fall out of coconut trees?

Trump: Yeah. No, I don't see it at all. But, the leaders of other countries—they are very competent. Putin, Xi—I can name every one of them. They're all very competent people. Most of them, almost all of them are at the top of their game. And we are playing checkers and they're playing chess.

Q: You are facing ninety-one criminal charges. And I think I have to say that if I think of anyone, not just in American politics now, but in the past, a normal person would just emotionally crumble. I mean, they'd go into the fetal position. They would. They would get out of the race. Not only have you not done that, but you seem to just forge relentlessly ahead. And what I want to ask you is, do you have a sort of inner fear that you have to overcome? How do you do it?

Trump: I don't know. A lot of people wouldn't be able to handle it. I can tell you, if I did that, I could get out of everything right now. I'd be able to get out of everything. They want to stop me. They don't care how they do it. And it's something that I think makes me stronger in a certain way. And I think that's not true with most people. Most people wouldn't do it. And it's horrible thing, but it bothers me much less than it would bother most people. I think it's probably helped me in terms of polls and everything else. The people see it. Normally that would be devastating for a poll, but this has helped me because they know it's a con job. It's a Democrat plot to fight against your opponent. It was started by Biden and also Kamala, the both of them, because she was a prosecutor. They started this in New York, in Atlanta, all of a sudden. I never had a problem like this in my life. All of a sudden I have like nine of these cases going on at one time. This is a political hoax and it's a sham.

Q: Is it a competitive impulse in you that goes, I'm just not going to let myself be defeated by it?

Trump: I just will not let myself be bothered by it. I want to go on and do what I have to do. I think they maybe regret that they did it because my poll numbers are much higher now than they have ever been. Normally your poll numbers would be down at nothing, but I have a platform for talking with people like you and others where I can talk about it, and when I talk about it, people understand it's all a hoax. It's all made up stuff.

Q: But what I mean is, you've done that. It's almost like you put them on trial. You were able to say, this is a sham, that the all these cases are ridiculous. "I made a perfectly reasonable phone call in Georgia." "You're saying overvalued Mar-a-Lago right here? Well . . ."

Trump: And then they value it at a tiny fraction of what the real value is. Think of it. These people will do anything. The whole thing is crazy. And look at what a guy like Biden did, where he says he's not going to give a country one billion dollars unless they change a prosecutor. And he said it on tape.

Q: Imagine if you said that.

Trump: If I said that, it's over. Look, I want to make this country strong and great. They just don't want to do that. They're very dishonest when it comes to campaigns. They're very dishonest when it comes to campaigning and, vote counting and everything, every aspect of dishonesty. And you have to win by a lot in order to win. And then we have to straighten out our election. So we can't have what happened in 2020 happen again.

Q: And will you assure the American people that if reelected, you will shut down this election fraud once and for all?

Trump: We're going to shut it down. We have to shut it down. We can't have these elections that go on for months and months, and you have stacked up in a corner of ballots and you have unsigned ballots. You have ballots that nobody knows where they came from. We can't have that. We have to have real elections. We need borders and we need elections. And then you need other things, too. But if you don't have borders and if you don't have elections, you're not going to have anything. So we have to have both. And we're going to have them.

Q: Let me ask you a question about this attempted assassination. You did an interview with Charlie Rose in the early nineties, and this was a difficult time for the company. You were facing all kinds of difficulties. You owed a lot of money. And Charlie Rose asked you, what are you most proud of? And you said, I'm most proud of the fact that I survived. But you said, I am also proud of the way I survived. And I flash forward now to this attempted assassin. And I say to myself, you survived. But it's not just you survived. It's the way you survived. And I think that's something that you couldn't prepare for. You couldn't rehearse for it, you couldn't put on an act. It is, it is you. What went through your mind?

Trump: Well, it was a very chilling moment. Surreal is a term you could use. I was in front of a massive, massive crowd of people and it was a lovely day, a little warm but lovely otherwise. And the sun was beaming and everything was good. And we had a crowd that the likes of which no candidate has ever had, you know, tens of thousands of people right in front of me and people behind me, too. But tens of thousands of people were there and I started. And the amazing thing is that I called out a chart on my right, which I never do, and if the chart wasn't used early, it would have been a different story.

Q: The Secret Service agents jumped on top of you. But something in you—I think you said, wait! And you, it's like you popped up. That's what I'm getting at. What made you do that?

Trump: Well, I wanted to get up and they had a stretcher, but I didn't want to be on a stretcher. And I felt it was my ear. I was pretty sure it was my ear, but there was blood all over the place. And the reason is that ears bleed the most. Can you believe that? The ears! Who would think so? I learn all sorts of things, but there was blood all over the place. They felt I was hit other places because of the fact that there was so much blood. But I wasn't. I said, I'm not. But I had seven or eight guys on top of me. This was not comfortable. And, I started, get me up. And I got up and I saw the fans. I saw the crowd. The patriots, they're incredible people, they didn't know: Was I hurt badly, or was I not hurt, or was I dead? They didn't know. They were confused. I could see it. But the amazing thing is that nobody ran. You know, if a bullet goes off in like a soccer stadium or anything, the people will run. They call it a stampede and people will get killed, but the people will run like crazy. Nobody ran. You saw that from the people behind me. It's like the opposite. They're looking around. They see what happened and they're looking around—some real incredible people, brave people. It was incredible to watch each face. There was nobody that ran because they saw that I was in trouble and they weren't going to leave. And I put up my fist and I said, fight, fight, fight. I don't know what it was exactly, but I said it. What a day.

Q: How has it changed you?

Trump: I don't know, I'm not sure that it changed me. People tell me, oh, it's changed you. Because it should have changed me. Because I'm, in theory, not supposed to be here doing an interview with you right now. I mean, I wouldn't be here, if my head wasn't in a certain position. It was literally in the only position it could be in. Pretty amazing.

Q: I thought of something Vivek Ramaswamy said. He said if Trump had been assassinated, America would have ended. I mean, what a statement to make. And it occurred to me that not only is there a providential hand on you, but to some degree a providential hand on America, which is what Washington believed and Lincoln believed. Do you believe it?

Trump: I think maybe so. And I think this was a good example of it, because, the odds of it happening like it happened where I'm here with you—and that took place a very short while ago—are tremendous odds. I mean, there's nobody who would take the bet. If you took the odds in Las Vegas and you put it on that, nobody would take that bet. So all I can say is, Yeah. It would have been a terrible thing for the country. It would have been a terrible thing for probably the world, in a sense. It was not a pleasant day, but it was maybe a day that something will come out of it that's going to be good for the future of this country.

Q: The Democrats have a horrible candidate. They've got horrible policies. Usually when you're in that situation, you think, how do I cheat? How do I cheat my way to victory? Now, I think it's probably fair to say that in different elections, the cheating isn't exactly the same. In 2020, they use one strategy, you know, the mules, in 2022, suddenly the tabulators don't work in Maricopa County, suppressing the Republican vote. And my question is, are you confident that between the Trump campaign, between the RNC, the new RNC, that you got your eyes on this election and that you'll be ready if the Democrats try to pull something.

Trump: You can never be too confident. I'd love to tell you I'm confident. But they cheat in many different ways. That's all they're good at. They're not good in policy. They're not good in government. They're not good running things. They're good at cheating in elections or they couldn't get in. You can't get in when you're in favor of open borders. You can't get in when you are in favor of things that are just so outlandish, so ridiculous. You know, no water coming out of your faucets, no water coming out of your shower. Men in women's sports. You have to use electric cars. You know, you can't win that way. You can't win. You win only by cheating. So when you say, are you confident, I don't even want to say that. I can say that we're working very hard and spending a lot of money on stopping it. And the one thing that is, and even that is not conclusive, but too big to rig is a statement that we use. But if you take a look at Pennsylvania, I was so far up in Pennsylvania, then all of a sudden I'm like tied. I said, what happened? Now I tell my people, don't help me with getting out the vote. We have all the votes we need. All I want you to do is guard the vote. When that vote comes in, make sure it's not swamped. It's not thrown out. Bad things don't happen. They don't drop ballots. And, as you know, this stuff happens. A lot of people don't know it. But as you know, it happens and it happens at levels that nobody's ever seen before. So now we have bad elections and we have bad borders. And those are the two things you have to have to have a great country. We don't have either. We're going to be focused very strongly, strongly on elections. But we have to get there first. We have to win. If we don't win, we can't fix that problem. We want to go to paper ballots. Do you know, paper ballots would cost 8 percent of what all of those fancy equipment costs. And they go out and they buy the most sophisticated equipment in the world. And then they say they'll have the election result in nine days! If you get paper ballots, they read it off that night. France had mail in a while ago and they had a lot of fraud. Any time you have mail in ballots, you're going to have massive fraud. And they went directly to paper ballots, so they had 38 million votes. It was all done by ten o'clock in the evening. And nobody complained. All paper ballots!

Q: I was going to ask you about this because one of the things that we expose in this film is that since we don't have any kind of marking on a ballot, it doesn't have a code, it doesn't have a watermark, you can actually buy ballots. And by that I mean you can buy the legitimate ballot paper from the very people who make it. Then you can then go online and get or even request an absentee ballot. You can then copy the absentee ballots onto the paper and you've got a ballot. Then you can just make copies and you got multiple ballots.

Trump: That's right. You're 100 percent right. But that's one of many things. People need to know we have very dishonest elections and we've got to straighten it out.

Q: There are going to be some Americans who have heard about the fraud, and they've heard about it going back now for a midterm election, the 2020 election. And they go, if the Democrats have got this heist down, that discourages me. I don't want to vote. What do we say to those people?

Trump: You got to get out and vote. We got to take back the system. Once we take back the system, we're going to fix it. We're going to fix it for good. But you have to get out and vote. If we vote, we're going to win. We're going to win. We have a lot of eyes open this time that we didn't have in 2020, and a lot of people are watching. It's much more difficult for them to do it. We're going to take back the system and we're going to fix our borders, and we're going to fix our elections.

Q: You're saying you'll do your part. You want them to do their part.
Trump: They have to do their part.

ENDNOTES

1. William Jennings Bryan, cited by Daniel J. Boorstin, *The Americans: The Democratic Experience* (New York: Vintage, 1974), p. 557.
2. Donald Trump, post on Truth Social, April 24, 2024; Brett Samuels, "Trump mocks Barr after endorsement, says he will remove 'lethargic' label," *The Hill*, April 25, 2024, thehill.com.
3. Donald Trump, post on Twitter, January 2, 2018.
4. Donald Trump, statement at Michigan rally, July 20, 2024.
5. Dana White, interview with Brian Kilmeade, "One Nation with Brian Kilmeade," June 18, 2024.
6. Dinesh D'Souza, *Stealing America* (New York: HarperCollins, 2015).
7. Winston Churchill, radio address to the nation, 1939, winstonchurchill.org.
8. Dinesh D'Souza, *Ronald Reagan: How an Ordinary Man Became an Extraordinary Leader* (New York: Macmillan, 1996).
9. Jeremy Diamond, "Trump: I could 'shoot somebody and I wouldn't lose voters,'" CNN, January 24, 2016, cnn.com.
10. Giselle Ruhiyyih Ewing, "Trump: I won't be a dictator 'except for day one,' *Politico*, May 5, 2023, politico.com.
11. Kristen Holmes, "Trump calls for the termination of the Constitution in Truth Social Post," CNN, December 4, 2022, cnn.com.
12. Mary Boykin Chesnut, *Mary Chesnut's Diary* (New York: Penguin, 2011).
13. Abraham Lincoln, "The Perpetuation of Our Political Institutions," Address to the Young Men's Lyceum of Springfield, Illinois, January 27, 1838, abrahamlincolnonline.org.
14. Abraham Lincoln, Message to the Special Session of Congress, July 4, 1861, millercenter.org.
15. Bret Stephens, "Lincoln Knew in 1838 What 2021 Would Bring," *New York Times*, January 19, 2021, nytimes.com; Jason Wilson, "Red Caesarism Is Rightwing Code—and Some Republicans Are Listening," *The Guardian*, October 1, 2023, theguardian.com.
16. Lincoln, Message to the Special Session of Congress, July 4, 1861.

17. Abraham Lincoln, remarks to the U.S. Sanitary Commission Fair, Baltimore, April 18, 1864, abrahamlincoln.org.

18. Harry Jaffa, *Crisis of the House Divided* (Chicago: University of Chicago Press, 1956), p. 218.

19. William Shakespeare, *Julius Caesar*, Act I, Scene II, Folger Shakespeare Library, folger.edu.

20. Donald Trump, *The Art of the Deal* (New York: Ballantine Books, 2015), pp. 47, 65.

21. Joseph Schumpeter, *The Entrepreneur* (Palo Alto, CA: Stanford University Press, 2011), p. 71.

22. Trump, *The Art of the Deal*, pp. 120–123, 137–138, 181–182.

23. Donald Trump, *The Art of the Comeback* (New York: Times Books, 1997), p. 11.

24. Dylan Matthews, "Zero-Sum Trump," *Vox*, January 19, 2017, vox.com.

25. Charlie Rose, Interview with Donald Trump, November 6, 1992, charlierose.com.

26. Cited by Gregory Cowles, "Inside the List," *New York Times*, November 13, 2015, nytimes.com.

27. Cited by Chris Cillizza, "Donald Trump's Interview with '60 Minutes' Was Eye-Opening. Also, Mike Pence Was There," *Washington Post*, July 18, 2016, washingtonpost.com.

28. Michael Kruse, "The 199 Most Donald Trump Things Donald Trump Has Ever Said," *Politico*, August 14, 2015, politico.com.

29. Donald Trump, post on Twitter, October 28, 2012.

30. Donald Trump, post on Twitter, August 28, 2012.

31. Karan Thapar, "Looking Back at Trump's Presidency Through His Tweets," *Hindustan Times*, November 16, 2020, hindustantimes.com.

32. John Cassidy, "What Myeshia Johnson Revealed about Donald Trump," *New Yorker*, October 24, 2017, newyorker.com.

33. Donald Trump, post on Twitter, July 19, 2012.

34. Kruse, "The 199 Most Donald Trump Things Donald Trump Has Ever Said."

35. Abraham Lincoln, "The Perpetuation of Our Political Institutions."

36. William Shakespeare, *Julius Caesar*, Act 1, Scene 1, Folger Shakespeare Library, folger.edu.

37. Id, Act 2, Scene 1.

38. Charlie Rose, interview with Donald Trump, November 6, 1992, charlierose.com

39. Michael Barbaro, "After Roasting, Trump Reacts in Character," *New York Times*, May 2, 2011, nytimes.com.

40. Donald Trump, post on Twitter, January 16, 2014.

41. Ben Jacobs, "Donald Trump on the Tonight Show: 'I Will Apologize…If I'm Ever Wrong,'" *The Guardian*, September 12, 2015, theguardian.com.

42. Donald Trump, post on Twitter, March 12, 2012.

43. Catherine Lucey and Steve Peoples, "Trump on John McCain: 'I Like People Who Weren't Captured,'" AP News, July 18, 2015, apnews.com.

44. Ellen Ucvhimiya, "Donald Trump Insults Carly Fiorina's Appearance," CBS News, September 10, 2015, cbsnews.com.

45. Rafi Schwartz, "74 Things Donald Trump Has Said About Women," *The Week*, July 22, 2024, theweek.com.

46. Tim Hains, "Trump: I Own A Store in Manhattan Worth More Than Mitt Romney," Real Clear Politics Video, March 3, 2016, realclearpolitics.com.

47. Michael Kruse, "In On the Joke," Politico, March 17, 2024, politico.com.

48. Fintan O'Toole, "Laugh Riot," *New York Review of Books*, March 21, 2024, nybooks.com.

49. Antonio Fins, "Five takeaways on what Trump said about locking up Hillary in 2016 campaign and thereafter," *The Palm Beach Post*, June 4, 2024, palmbeachpost.com.

50. Jill Filipovic, "Stormy Daniels, Feminist Hero," *New York Times*, August 24, 2018, nytimes.com.

51. German Lopez, "Donald Trump's long history of racism, from the 1970s to 2020," Vox, August 13, 2020, vox.com.

52. "Full text: Trump's comments on white supremacists, 'alt-left' in Charlottesville," Politico, August 15, 2017, politico.com.

53. Curt Reiss, *Joseph Goebbels* (London: Fonthill, 2015), p. 64–65.

54. Dante, *The Divine Comedy* (New York: Penguin Books, 1984), Vol. I: Inferno, p. 318.

55. Shawn Snow and Howard Altman, "Trump Says al-Baghdadi 'died like a dog' in US commando raid in Syria," *Army Times*, October 27, 2019, armytimes.com.

56. George Orwell, *1984* (New York: Signet Classics, 1977), p. 267.

57. William Shakespeare, *Julius Caesar*, Act III, Scene II, Folger Shakespeare Library, folger.edu.

58. Aleksandr Solzhenitsyn, *The Gulag Archipelago* (London: The Harvill Press, 1985), p. x.

59. Cited by A. James Gregor, *Giovanni Gentile: Philosopher of Fascism* (New Brunswick: Transaction Publishers, 2008), p. 63.

60. Solzhenitsyn, *The Gulag Archipelago*, pp. x, 4, 43.

61. Vaclav Havel, "The Power of the Powerless," December 23, 2011, hac.bard.edu.

62. Orwell, *1984*, p. 208.

63. George Orwell, letter to Noel Willmett, 1944, thedailybeast.com.

64. E. A. Ross, *Social Control* (New York: Macmillan, 1918), pp. 74, 82.

65. "Mr. Obama has told people that it would be easier to be the president of China." Mark Landler and Helene Cooper, "Obama Seeks a Course

of Pragmatism in the Middle East," *New York Times*, March 10, 2011, nytimes.com.

66. Joe Concha, "Jane Fonda Calls Coronavirus 'God's Gift to the Left,'" *The Hill*, October 7, 2020, thehill.com.

67. Michael Barone, "The Proximal Origins of a Scientific Fraud," American Enterprise Institute, July 26, 2023, aei.org.

68. Jim Geraghty, "Fauci: 'It Sort of Just Appeared, That Six Feet Is Going to Be the Distance,'" *National Review*, June 3, 2024, nationalreview.com.

69. Joseph Guzman, "CDC Reverses Statement by Director That Vaccinated People Are No Longer Contagious," *The Hill*, April 5, 2021, thehill.com.

70. Charlie Warzel, "Don't Go Down the Rabbit Hole," *New York Times*, February 18, 2021, nytimes.com.

71. Trevor Aaronson, "Echoes of FBI Entrapment Haunt Failed Plot to Kidnap Gretchen Whitmer," *The Intercept*, March 9, 2022, theintercept.com.

72. Lorraine Boissoneault, "The True Story of the Reichstag Fire and the Nazi Rise to Power," *Smithsonian*, February 21, 2017, smithsonianmag.com.

73. Jonathan Lemire and Robert Burns, "Milley defends calls to Chinese as effort to avoid conflict," AP, September 15, 2021, apnews.com.

74. William Shakespeare, *Macbeth*, Act III, Scene IV, Folger Shakespeare Library, folger.edu.

75. Joe Biden, post on X, June 28, 2024; Tim Hains, "Pelosi: This is Not a Normal Election, Trump Must Be Stopped," July 2, 2024, realclearpolitics.com.

76. Joe Ciardiello, "The Case for Political Exile for Donald Trump," Politico, November 13, 2020, politico.com; Kirk Swearingen, "Can we send Trump into exile? It worked (sort of) with Napoleon," Salon, January 28, 2024, salon.com.

77. AP, "Banker Involved in Big Loans to Trump's Company Testifies for His Defense in Civil Fraud Trial," November 28, 2023, usnews.com.

78. J. Michael Luttig and Laurence H. Tribe, "The Constitution Prohibits Trump From Ever Being President Again," *The Atlantic*, August 19, 2023, theatlantic.com.

79. J. Michael Luttig and Laurence H. Tribe, "Supreme Betrayal," *The Atlantic*, March 14, 2024, theatlantic.com.

80. Transcript, "Highlights of Trump's Call with the Georgia Secretary of State," *New York Times*, January 3, 2021, nytimes.com.

81. AP, "DNC, Clinton campaign agree to Steele dossier funding fine," March 31, 2022, apnews.com.

82. Post by @AlexanderSoros on X, May 31, 2024.

83. Scott Adams @ScottAdams Says, post on X, July 14, 2024.

84. Dave Goldiner, "Bullet like 'world's largest mosquito,' Trump tells RFK, Jr.," *Boston Herald*, July 16, 2024, bostonherald.com.

85. David Frum, "The Gunman and the Would-Be Dictator," *The Atlantic*, July 14, 2024, theatlantic.com.

86. Christopher Klein, "When Teddy Roosevelt Was Shot in 1912, a Speech May Have Saved His Life," July 15, 2024, history.com.

87. Lorraine Smith Pangle, "The Anatomy of Courage in Aristotle's *Nicomachean Ethics*," *The Review of Politics* 80 (2018), pp. 569–590.

88. Joseph Stalin, 1923, quoted in Boris Bazhanov, *The Memoirs of Stalin's Former Secretary*, OxfordReference.com.

89. Molly Ball, "The Secret History of the Shadow Campaign That Saved the 2020 Election," *Time*, February 4, 2021, time.com.

90. Ali Swenson, "Fact Focus: Gaping holes in the claim of 2K ballot 'mules,'" AP, May 3, 2022, apnews.com.

91. Stuart A. Thompson and Charlie Warzel, "One Nation, Tracked," *New York Times*, December 20, 2019, nytimes.com.

92. Rasmussen Reports, "'2000 Mules': Documentary's Message Resonates With Voters—Demographic Details," rasmussenreports.com.

93. Rasmussen Reports, "One in Five Mail-In Voters Admit They Cheated in 2020 Election," December 12, 2023, rasmussenreports.com.

94. Shania Shelton, Maricopa County, "Investigation into printer issues during 2022 election finds 'equipment failure' at fault," CNN, April 11, 2023, cnn.com.

95. Josh Christenson, "How non-citizens are getting voter registration forms across the US—and how Republicans are trying to stop it," *New York Post*, June 14, 2024, nypost.com.

96. Alexander Hamilton, James Madison and John Jay, *The Federalist* (NY: Barnes and Noble Classics, 2006), pp. 151–152.

97. Lord Charnwood, *Abraham Lincoln* (Mineola, NY: Dover Publications, 1997), p. 167.

98. Dante, *The Divine Comedy*, Vol. I: Inferno, pp. 379–383.

99. William Shakespeare, *Julius Caesar*, Act I, Scene III, Folger Shakespeare Library, folger.edu.

100. William Shakespeare, *Coriolanus*, Act IV, Scene V, Folger Shakespeare Library, folger.edu.

101. Eric Bradner, "Bush: 'I'm worried that I will be the last Republican president," CNN, July 19, 2016, cnn.com.

102. Friedrich Nietzsche, *Thus Spoke Zarathustra* (New York: Penguin Books, 1978), pp. 169–170.

103. Leo Strauss, *Natural Right and History* (Chicago: University of Chicago Press, 1953), pp. 157–159.

104. Dinesh D'Souza, *The End of Racism* (New York: The Free Press, 1995).

105. Geraldo Cadava, "The Rise of Latino White Supremacy," *New Yorker*, May 30, 2023, newyorker.com; NPR, "Understanding Multiracial Whiteness and Trump Supporters," a conversation between Lulu Garcia-Navarro and Christina Beltran, January 24, 2021, npr.org.

106. See, e.g., Mike Davis, post on X, June 7, 2024.

107. 18 U.S.C. 241 and 18 U.S.C. 242, U.S. Department of Justice, justice.gov.

108. Abraham Lincoln, Order of Retaliation, Executive Order, July 30, 1863, teachingamericanhistory.org.

109. Charlie Savage, Reid J. Epstein, Maggie Haberman and Jonathan Swan, "The Resistance to a New Trump Administration Has Already Started," *New York Times*, June 16, 2024, nytimes.com.